BIG little house

What are the challenges architects face when designing dwelling spaces of a limited size? And what can these projects tell us about architecture—and architectural principles—in general?

In *BIG little house*, award-winning architect Donna Kacmar introduces 20 real-life examples of small houses. Each project is under 1,000 square feet (100 square meters) in size and, brought together, the designs reveal an attitude towards materiality, light, enclosure, and accommodation which is unique to minimal dwellings. The book demonstrates that while they are part of a trend to address growing concerns about minimizing consumption and lack of affordable housing, small dwellings are not always simply the result of budget constraints but constitute a deliberate design strategy in their own right.

Highly illustrated and in full colour throughout, each example is based on interviews with the original architect and accompanied by detailed floor plans. This groundbreaking, beautifully designed text offers practical guidance to any professional architect or homeowner interested in small-scale projects.

Donna Kacmar is a practicing architect and an Associate Professor at the Gerald D. Hines College of Architecture at the University of Houston, USA, where she teaches Comprehensive Design Studio and directs the Materials Research Collaborative.

'When it comes to houses, quality, not quantity, is what truly matters. Architect Donna Kacmar's eloquently written and beautifully illustrated *BIG little house* underscores this point again and again. The book's comprehensive introduction coupled with twenty carefully curated examples answer not just "what" but also "how" and "why". *BIG little house* is a valuable resource for architects and clients alike.'   **Naomi Pollock, AIA, author of *Modern Japanese House*, Japan**

'A rigorous examination of the history of the small house is presented in both sumptuous photography and in floor plans at comparative scales, which are both useful and very revealing. Common to all of the houses is an attention to the importance of detail in small spaces, the importance of opening to the exterior to borrow space from the landscape, and the belief in quality over quantity, an idea that should guide all residential design in an era of diminishing resources.'   **Mark McInturff, FAIA, architect, McInturff Architects, USA**

BIG little house

Small houses designed by architects

Donna Kacmar

Routledge
Taylor & Francis Group

LONDON AND NEW YORK

First published 2015
by Routledge
2 Park Square, Milton Park, Abingdon, Oxon OX14 4RN

and by Routledge
711 Third Avenue, New York, NY 10017

Routledge is an imprint of the Taylor & Francis Group, an informa business

British Library Cataloguing-in-Publication Data
A catalogue record for this book is available from the British Library

Library of Congress Cataloging in Publication Data
Kacmar, Donna.
BIG little house : small houses designed by architects / Donna Kacmar.
pages cm
Includes bibliographical references and index.
1. Small houses. 2. Architect-designed houses. I. Title.
NA7533.K33 2015
728--dc23
2014027232

ISBN: (hbk) 978-1-138-02419-9
ISBN: (pbk) 978-1-138-02420-5
ISBN: (ebk) 978-1-138-77593-7

Typeset in Myriad Pro by
Servis Filmsetting Ltd, Stockport, Cheshire

Cover images and photographers

Top row (left to right): Watershed, J. Gary Tarleton; Music Box, John Grable and Matt Martinez; False Bay Writer's Cabin, Tim Bies;
Ravine Guest House, Raimund Koch.

Second row (left to right): Writer's Studio, Elliot Kaufman; Hill Country Jacal, Leigh Christian; Kemper Cabin, David Story;
Marfa 10x10, Chris Cooper.

Third row (left to right): Keenan Tower House, Timothy Hursley; Sky Ranch, Benjamin Benschneider; Scholar's Library, Paul Warchol;
Roland Cabin, Peter Bastianelli-Kerze.

Fourth row (left to right): Small House in an Olive Grove, Elliot Kaufman; Stacked Cabin, John J. Macaulay; Williams Cabin,
Mark Williams; Craven Road Studio, Finn O'Hara.

Bottom row (left to right): Pool House, Eric Staudenmaier; Blossom Street 03, Nash Baker; Nested House, Luis Ayala;
Envelope House, Nic Lehoux.

Contents

Variant ONE: Porous Dwellings

Variant TWO: Focused Dwellings

Variant THREE: Protected Dwellings

List of Illustrations

Foreword

During a recent trip to Switzerland, I finally got to visit the house that Le Corbusier designed for his parents on the shores of Lake Geneva. The small but seminal work known as "Le Lac" (1923–24) had intrigued me ever since I learned about it in a modern architecture history class. In particular, I treasured an iconic image of the house: a still life composed of a tabletop and chairs next to an ivy-encrusted stone wall with an opening overlooking the lake and mountains. Embracing this timeless composition was an ancient tree that, year round, cast its alchemy of leaves and shadows. Everything about Le Lac was encapsulated in the serenity of this image: an outdoor room delineated by precise proportions that amplified the experience of place. This is the image I had in mind when crossing the house's street gate and threshold, thus my surprise to find the marvelous tree gone and the stone wall cleansed of any ivy, plastered over and painted blistering white. The "restorer" of this new phase of Le Lac greeted us and gave us a tour while proudly stating that he had brought the house back to its original state (a delusional pronouncement if I ever heard one). Yet disappointment aside, the house and grounds exerted the spell of its carefully constructed universe. For a moment I could imagine Le Corbusier's mother sitting by the table on a balmy afternoon, delighting in the hypnotic effect of light rippling across the lake's surface.

Le Lac is an intimate work with immense cumulative power: a "big little house." That same force inhabits the collection of houses in Donna Kacmar's book. Her compilation is not only an ode to the innumerable marvels found in big little houses but a welcome and timely reflection on their meanings, especially when considering the distressed state of the single-family houses that are marketed across the globe today. We see suburbs as well as inner-city streets overtaken by houses that trade on their distorted proportions and historicist concoctions with impunity. These houses do not just mirror unmitigated consumption, they also drain the vital strength of the house as a critical tool for living. Thus the house as an investigation on how to live has been overturned by designs that offer little in return but oversized square footage with a

high deficit of experiential quality. Excessive square footage fueled by fast and furious construction adds little to the enjoyment of space or the experience of its daily rituals.

Thus the need for the big little house to remind us of how little we might need to live with or how much pleasure this realization ultimately brings to our experience of the world. We discover that in their economy of means the houses in this book practice the utmost generosity and delight, their immediacy and tactility becoming a daily ritual of discovery. These big little houses also bring us closer to the architect's key design principles or sensibilities, as can be seen in Shim-Sutcliffe's Ravine Guest House and Craven Road Studio, or in Peter Gluck's Scholar's Library, or in David Salmela's Roland Cabin, to name just a few of the houses featured. We take pleasure in each architect's attention to the minutiae of a detail, the clarity of an idea, the sustaining pleasure of a material, or simply the framing of a view. More importantly, we come to understand that in the fortitude of each house's circumstances lies that which "inspires a larger architecture."

Thirty years ago I built my own big little house, and for some years I inhabited a kind of haven; or more precisely I lived in a work sculpted by time, a work where everything from a pecan tree, a north-facing window to a library tower slowed the rapid passage of time, even when at its most ephemeral. I discovered in designing and building this small work that architecture is time constructed by the intricate tenses that map its circular course. The mystery and wonder of architecture resides in this intimate circumference of time, even more apparent in the luxurious compactness that a big little house provides regardless of its shape, cost, or location. For much like a carefully made watch encased in its protective matching form, you open its lid and enter not the drumbeat of time but the unfolding of its inimitable composition—at times near, at times distant or forgotten, but always at the reach of one's hand.

Carlos Jimenez   05/15/14

Preface

My interest in small houses began with the design of my own home. Modesty in size was pursued directly out of necessity; a small budget only affords building something of a limited scope. I experimented with some very "straightforward"— another word for inexpensive—materials that were not appropriate to "try out" on real clients. As my simply sealed construction-grade pine plywood floors have softly darkened over the years, I now have confidence using that material for a client's floor. Large panels of cementitious boards, with joints hidden by battens, clad the exterior. The detail was developed after the contractor said "you cannot afford the person who can install that straight." In my own home of limited square feet, any one material or assembly technique that might fail could easily be reworked or replaced. Over the past twenty years, designing large houses, as well as commercial and institutional projects, I have learned a lot, yet much of my architectural practice and research has focused on modest dwellings.

Five years ago, I was asked to design a small lake house. The final house, with a zigzag-shaped plan, defines an equal amount of indoor and outdoor living space. The client requested views of the lake to the east and privacy from neighboring houses. The bedroom and the living room are pulled from a simple compact volume that houses the bath, kitchen, and support spaces, allowing for the separation of the sleeping area from the more active spaces and providing maximum privacy within the minimal volume. Energy- and resource-efficient windows, doors, equipment, fixtures, and appliances reinforce the (literally) small footprint of the house. Other sustainable strategies include careful siting and orientation to take advantage of natural ventilation and daylight. Existing trees help shade the building and several outdoor shaded spaces are part of the program. New material use was kept to a minimum on the interior. Recycled glass slabs were used for kitchen and bath countertops and for the

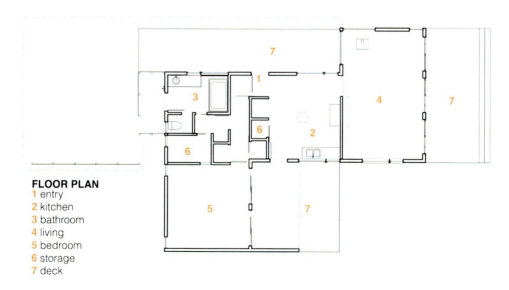

FLOOR PLAN
1 entry
2 kitchen
3 bathroom
4 living
5 bedroom
6 storage
7 deck

Figure P.1 Lake House 98 floor plan

Figure P.2 Lake House 98 view from kitchen looking into living room

tub surround. A gas range and wood chopping block, which have both been in the client's family for generations, were refurbished.

More recently, a client asked me to design a truly small house. He originally wanted to live near his work and grandchildren in his 34-foot-long Airstream trailer on a piece of residential property he has owned for years. When the city would not allow him to hook up his trailer to utilities, we investigated multiple options to determine how he could leave his expensive downtown condominium and find a good temporary housing situation until he retired to Austin to live full-time. The construction budget was determined by simply multiplying his years until retirement by the annual condo association fees he was currently paying. The house dimensions were influenced by the module of the existing Airstream trailer and the maximum dimensions of a building that could be moved on a highway. The house sits on piers, allowing the tie-down metal straps to be cut and the house to be easily placed on a truck for transport to a property in the Texas Hill Country if a future owner buys the lot for land value only. To allow for a new larger

main house to be built in the center if desired by the new owner, we placed the 544-square-foot house at the very back of the 90 feet by 220 feet city lot. The existing modest dwelling could then become a guest house or rowdy teenage pad.

A carport, which can act as a porch, and a large Ipe wood deck sit next to the small house, enlarging the livable space and looking out to the landscaped lawn. The house is wrapped in low-maintenance metal siding with hidden fasteners on the exterior. Simple, nontoxic materials are used inside to satisfy the chemical sensitivity of the owner. The bathroom and closet are clad in salvaged white oak siding that matches the kitchen cabinetry and reflects the cabin-like quality of this very modest home. Two sliding panels of marine-grade plywood close down the house while the owner is away or when a hurricane is brewing in the Gulf of Mexico.

After completing these two projects, I began to look at small dwellings not only as something defined by budget constraints but also as a design interest. I searched for what could be learned about architecture when there is limited

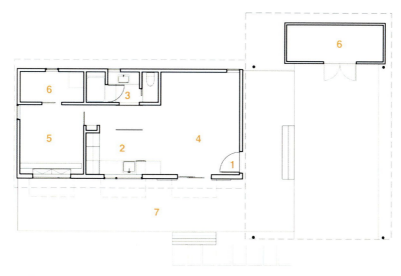

FLOOR PLAN
1 entry
2 kitchen
3 bathroom
4 living
5 bedroom
6 storage
7 deck or patio

Figure P.3 Fisher Street House floor plan

Figure P.4 Fisher Street House looking into living room from front door

Figure P.5 Crane Island Cabin by Wendell Lovett, FAIA

space with which to work. This interest in modest dwellings may be a family trait. My parents remember admiring, while visiting the Pacific Northwest in the mid-1980s, a small vacation house they saw on Crane Island. They later learned that Wendell Lovett, FAIA, designed the house. They wrote the architect a note and sent him a check. He soon mailed back two sheets of construction drawings for the house.[1] When talking to my father about this book idea he jumped up, walked over to his files, and pulled out a manila envelope with those blueprints still inside. I soon began my conversations with the architects and homeowners whose stories are inside this book.

Note

1 Wendell Lovett built the Crane Island retreat for his family in 1970. The simple shelter is built from prefabricated elements that, when bolted together on-site, form triangular trusses. The trusses allow the wood deck to cantilever from the foundation and hover over the south-facing rocky beach in the middle of the San Juan Islands, providing views to the sky and sea. My parents never built the small house by Wendell Lovett, and after about ten years, they asked me to design the house they currently live in.

Acknowledgements

I am grateful for the architects, their clients, and their photographers who were generous with project images and with their time during interviews and phone calls and in writing emails. This book would not be possible without their willingness to share stories and insights. I learned so much about being an architect from each of them.

I am indebted to the help of many others as well.

Dean Patricia Oliver, the College of Architecture, and the University of Houston granted faculty development leave and financial support that allowed me the necessary time and resources to complete this book.

Carlos Jimenez, who graciously wrote the foreword, inspired me as a young designer to build my own house. His little house on Willard Street serves as a testament to the act of daring that embodies all architecture.

Daniel Friedman encouraged me to write about this topic several years ago when he saw my Fisher Street House published. He also introduced me to the work of several of the architects included in this book. I am grateful for his confidence in this project.

Canan Yetmen was my independent editor. I relied heavily on her help, counsel, and thoughtful review.

Alejandra Cervantes, an architecture student at the University of Houston, skillfully redrew each site plan, floor plan, and section to the same scale and drawing style so each building could be readily understood and easily compared. Each site plan is at 1 inch equals 50 feet scale and each floor plan and section is at 1 inch equals 16 feet scale (except where noted otherwise in the case of the Long Skinny House With a Kink in It).

I am thrilled to be working with Alanna Donaldson, Fran Ford, Grace Harrison, and Jennifer Schmidt at Routledge. They have supported me during the entire process and have been a pleasure to work with. I cannot describe the excitement I felt when, as a first-time author, I received confirmation of Routledge's interest in the book.

I am thankful for my family, friends, and colleagues who gracefully reviewed my work and often sent me comments or examples of small houses. Both Jerry Maffei and Bruce Webb read earlier drafts and offered critical insights. Cindy Kacmar, Diane Kacmar, and Steve Kacmar offered support and proofreading skills. Without the help of everyone listed above and Natalye Appel, Jeffrey Brown, Rusty Bienvenue, Sharon Chapman, Judith De Jong, Jean Krchnak, Karen Lantz, Brian Malarkey, and Danny Samuels the book would not be the same!

Introduction

German philosopher Martin Heidegger described dwelling as the way in which humans spend their time "wandering" between birth and death, on earth and under the sky. More recently, the influential American architect Charles Moore wrote:

> One of the basic human requirements is the need to dwell, and one of the central human acts is the act of inhabiting, of connecting ourselves, however temporarily, with a place on the planet that belongs to us, and to which we belong.[1]

Architects often refer back to the mythic "first dwelling" when designing a house. This first dwelling provided "protection against inclement weather, wild beasts and human enemies," according to architect and historian Banister Fletcher.[2] Novelist Junichiro Tanizaki, in his book *In Praise of Shadows*, also argues that the first shelter for Easterners was a "parasol" roof that provided a place to "throw a shadow on the earth."[3] He explains that Westerners first provided a roof for shelter from rain and weather while Easterners were most interested in keeping the sun out of buildings. Regardless of what we are sheltering ourselves from, we are able to be more relaxed and experience the act of dwelling when we feel physically and psychologically secure. Enclosing structures have the "capacity to transform us from anxious victims to secure observers."[4] Providing a specific sense of shelter and protection is a clear goal in the twenty buildings included in this volume. Some are porous and provide the minimal shelter required. Others are open only in specific ways. Many form a thick protective skin around the inhabitants.

In addition, each of the twenty projects takes a slightly different turn at what it might require to dwell in a more poetic way. French philosopher Gaston Bachelard describes our house as our own corner of the world, a place for integration of thoughts, memories, and dreams. Bachelard's ideas are made physical in these small projects; each takes a specific attitude towards what it means to dwell in a particular place. These projects are both tuned to their sites and to their particular programmatic requirements. The sites range from very rural to suburban or urban sites. Some of the buildings provide a space for a particular activity, and others are full-time residences. All of the projects are small, yet they each have very big ideas about how materials and light work together to accommodate and enclose the inhabitants.

The current interest in small dwellings is noted in recent articles in *Dwell* magazine, the *New York Times*, and other national publications. Many cities in North America are encouraging smaller living units. In New York City, nARCHITECTS—the winner of the adAPT design competition—is creating the city's first "micro-unit" apartment building with units that range in size from 275 to 300 square feet. In Vancouver, Bruce Carscadden is designing 250-square-foot "micro lofts." Also in Vancouver, the new Laneway Housing program allows small units—between 500 and 850 square feet—to be built along the alleys of existing houses. Diane Sugimura with the City of Seattle is working on legislation that reduces lot size and allows micro-housing and accessory dwelling units in the growing city. Boneyard Studios, founded in 2012, is building small infill houses in Washington DC as well as influencing local building codes in the nation's capital. Even in Texas, where big is often seen as being better, private developers are interested in building smaller housing units and catering to a new market. In Houston, a local developer is looking at building speculative small houses for young professionals, and on the beach near Galveston, Chula Ross Sanchez just completed three new 700-square-foot LEED-certified dwellings, Las Casitas, replacing the original 1930s cottages destroyed by Hurricane Ike in 2008.

This evolution of smaller dwellings is also affected by overall housing affordability, cost and availability of land, and changing bank appraisal standards. Bob Ransford, an urban design specialist in Vancouver, finds a

> disconnect between the housing we are currently supplying—especially in suburban areas where the single-family detached home is the desired typology—and the housing that is missing but that would meet our needs.[5]

Affordability and changing lifestyles have led to a greater acceptance of smaller dwelling units for baby boomers, a generation that remembers growing up in smaller houses. This trend of increased support for smaller dwelling units from municipal governments and developers is matched by the realization that smaller dwellings can help low-income, middle-income, and even homeless populations find needed shelter at a reasonable cost.

There is also a general interest in a "reduction" lifestyle in lieu of a "consumption" lifestyle. Reduction is a way to simplify a complicated modern life. Concerns regarding sustainability, financial health of retirement portfolios, or even the ability to pursue alternative life paths can lead to minimizing the investments we make in physical things. Websites such as LifeEdited.com encourage a lifestyle of leanness and show how to "live large in small spaces." The website highlights spaces, products, and systems that facilitate life simplification.

Along similar lines, the "tiny house movement" is a "do-it-yourself" trend, with a series of books, organizations, workshops, and websites devoted to minimal living for both environmental and financial reasons. These "tiny" houses are often between 100 and 400 square feet. The movement's popular website, thetinylife.com, makes the argument that after thirty years of paying for financing, taxes, and maintenance, the real cost of a modest $300,000 house mushrooms to over one million dollars. It acknowledges that the effort and the time required to accumulate that amount of money might be better spent in other ways.

In North America, the home—particularly the single-family house—remains part dream and part rational investment. The home provides our basic human need for shelter and is also connected to our values and emotions. Even though the average size of a new house in the United States continues to increase, some homeowners are interested in efficiency and architects have been designing small houses for many generations. Today's interest in efficient living can be traced back to earlier examples of houses designed to be modest while accommodating the modern lifestyles of occupants.

The history of the house could begin in the seventeenth century when the home became a place of refuge and privacy. Before this, the house was often encumbered with public functions, workshops, and housing of animals along with providing living space for family members. Changes within society continue to shape our notions of home. Evolution of technology and lifestyle, for example, influence how we can connect for conversation, to listen to the radio, or to watch a flat-screen television with ample space for a PlayStation. The hearth, traditionally the center of the house, is no longer required; thermal comfort is provided by hidden machines. The kitchen, once segregated due to safety concerns, now includes spaces for eating and is directly connected to other areas of the house. Bathing facilities and toilets have also moved from being outside to becoming integrated into the home's living areas. Today houses include "usage neutral rooms" that can accommodate all of the functions of living rather than being designed only for specific activities of eating, sleeping, working, or bathing.

When we look to the past for instructions on modest dwellings, Steven Holl reminds us of many vernacular examples—the one-room house, the stack house, the saddlebag house (straddling a central fireplace), the dogtrot house—and the efficiency that each offered in its geometric rigor.[6] Each starts with a simple central core space that can accommodate multiple activities with appendages that can be added over time in order to support specific activities or increased spatial needs. These are examples of homes that are able to move "beyond merely meeting the demands of their first inhabitants,"[7] and they can be seen as very unselfconscious buildings that are "symbols of humanity at a very simple level."[8]

Architects and developers explored modest, efficient dwellings both before and right after World War II. Irving Gill's Workman Three-Room Cottages in Southern California, Gerrit Rietveld's

Figure I.1 Glass House by Philip Johnson

Schröder House of 1924 in Utrecht, and Rudolph Schindler's Lake Arrowhead retreat of 1934 are all early examples of individual small homes. Experiments in modest dwellings were happening at a larger scale as well. The popular Sears Modern Homes (1908–40), Buckminster Fuller's circular Dymaxion Deployment Unit (1929), Lustron prefabricated enameled steel houses of 1947, the small 800-square-foot houses of Levittown (1947), and the California Case Study House program reflect an interest in exploring efficiency. Architects were also designing small houses for themselves and, sometimes, their clients.

In North America, two small iconic modern houses—the Glass House by Philip Johnson and the Farnsworth House by Mies van der Rohe—serve as touchstones for contemporary architects. Both use a steel frame structural system and large planes of glass to separate the interior space from the exterior. The Glass House, built in 1949, is a single rectangular space enclosed by a thin skin of glass and steel. The dark steel columns are placed on the interior of the glass, rendering

a smooth exterior surface. The rectangular building is three structural bays long and sits solidly on a concrete slab covered in a herringbone pattern of dark brick pavers. The ceramic flooring gives more visual weight to the small box and connects it solidly to the earth. Only the cylindrical brick enclosure of the bathroom and fireplace penetrates the roof or interrupts interior space. The kitchen, a small collection of low cabinetry, is placed off to one side near the entry. The building is part of a collection of small buildings designed by Johnson on the large wooded property in New Haven, Connecticut.

Mies' Farnsworth House, built in 1951 in Plano, Illinois, floats over the gently sloping ground plane near the often unruly Fox River with which it aligns. Wide steps lead from the ground to a large terrace and then to the porch, covered by an extension of the house roof. All horizontal decks are lifted off the ground in an attempt to be out of the floodplain, defying gravity and conveying a visual lightness to the structure. The white painted structural steel "cage" is placed on the outside

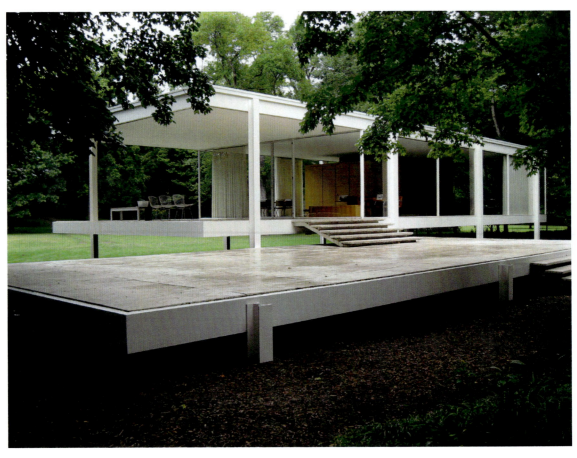

Figure I.2 Farnsworth House by Mies van der Rohe

of the glass. Steel flange vertical members extend past the cornice of the roof at the top and run straight down to the concrete footings at the ground. The utilities, bathrooms, storage, fireplace, and kitchen are housed in a solid enclosure, placed off-center in the plan and clad in vertical grain wood. A continuous curtain runs along the inside face of the uninterrupted glass wall to provide privacy or allow the occupant to define specific views between fabric panels. Both the Glass House and the Farnsworth House elegantly demonstrate the architectural power of a small building.

Le Corbusier, the preeminent twentieth-century architect, was interested in the efficiently designed small house as documented in his early projects such as the Maison des Péons, Le Faucheur Housing Units, housing at Pessac, and Villa Le Lac, a house he designed for his mother on the lake near Lausanne, Switzerland. The weekend house he designed in 1952, Cabanon located in Roquebrune-Cap-Martin, France, is most certainly a "machine for living" in which everyday functions are supported

but nothing extraneous is included. The project originated as a birthday present for his wife Yvonne. Though the plan was derived from the steel-framed Maison Loucheur of 1928, the *cabanon* was essentially a log cabin built from sectioned pine logs with an interior of prefabricated plywood panels that were built in Corsica and transported by boat, train, and eventually hand-carried to the site. Le Corbusier investigated the construction technique and cabin organization, which drew inspiration from simple Mediterranean houses, as a prototype for a mass-produced vacation cabin. Le Corbusier's interest in proportion and modularity is revealed in this small house of just 144 square feet. The main unit is appended with a bathroom and a small entry corridor.

In the fifteen square meters of the *cabanon*, in the shade of a great Carob tree, Le Corbusier arranged everything necessary for rest and work, with no element other than the essential, but also with all that was superfluous that is indispensable to the happiness of man.[9]

Figure I.3 Cabanon by Le Corbusier

Included among the items "indispensable to the happiness of man" and designed specifically for the efficient space are the stainless steel sink inspired by one he saw on a plane to India, the wooden handles on the cabinets derived from the Unité d'Habitation in Marseilles, the painted plywood storage panels in the ceiling, and the thin vertical windows—*aerateurs*—for cross ventilation. The windows are equipped with shutters that are faced with a mirror on the inner surface which reflects the exterior landscape. These shutters are functional and aesthetic; while the *cabanon* has an interior constructed materiality that is clearly distinct and not related to its exterior shell, the reflected images of the landscape reconnect the occupant to the exterior and the sea. As noted by Claude Prelorenzo, there is a direct "contrast between the sheen of the interior and the ruggedness of the exterior."[10]

A big painted mural, the yellow painted wood floor, the white, red, blue, and green ceiling panels with hidden storage, and the fixed partitions and moveable furniture on casters animate the interior. An office space inside faces the sea, with shelving placed to one side for ease of access from the desk. Furniture was designed as heavy boxes using a combination of

hardwoods and plywood. The solid chestnut wood headboard and the storage *tabouret* reflect Le Corbusier's interest in elemental furniture as well as flexibility of use. The interior surfaces of the *cabanon* are interactive; the shelves, openings in the cuboid space dividers, light fixtures, batten joints in plywood cladding, clothes closet with arranged knobs, sliding panels, and the mirrored shutters are both useful and artistic expressions. The "ornament is sparse and directly related to the craft of working the materials in which it occurs."[11] In this small dwelling, much care and attention was given to the craft of architecture and the experience of the inhabitants. Le Corbusier famously stated: "I am so happy with my *cabanon* that I shall doubtless end my days here."[12]

In the United States, during the mid-1950s, Paul Rudolph and the Sarasota School of architects were designing small houses on the west coast of Florida. Rudolph's Cocoon House, designed with collaborator Ralph Twitchell, sits alongside a canal, now almost hidden among the newer much larger "dream vacation" homes. In 1949 it stood alone, a simple elevated wood structure with a concave roof made from an experimental and very thin fiberglass membrane held

Figure I.4 Cocoon House by Paul Rudolph and Ralph Twitchell

in tension. Steel cables connect the roof to the wood floor system outriggers. The house is composed of four structural bays. Three of the bays comprise the main living area with an adjacent small office. The fourth bay is reserved for the private zone of the house and includes a small bedroom and bath. An entrance deck on the street side leads visitors to the kitchen area. A similar deck cantilevers on the canal side and has a built-in seat for perching over the water. Rudolph later critiqued his own design: he felt the downward force of the concave roof encouraged occupants to move towards the exterior and that, instead, "a house should draw occupants inside."[13] The end wall in the living space has one large sliding glass panel that focuses views down the canal.

Building experimentation was occurring on both the west and east coasts of Florida. On the state's east coast, Alfred Browning Parker designed several modest houses including a

house for his own family in 1943 and the Ewing Residence of 1955, both in Coconut Grove. Although he was born in Boston in 1916, his family moved to Florida for young Alfred's health in 1925, and Parker spent much of his professional life working in the subtropical humidity. While he worked on large residential and commercial projects, Parker also designed modest homes for middle-class families, including one for a house painter and another for a postman. His work has been noted for its

engagement and enhancement of the environment … forthright expression of construction, engagement of local building traditions, authenticity of materials, and the use of natural materials from the region … spatial freedom combined with sense of place.[14]

The Ewing Residence of 1955, a 26 foot by 26 foot square lifted out of the storm surge, on grey block columns, has a

Figure I.5 Ewing House by Alfred Browning Parker

rather dramatic promenade entrance. A long ramp doubles back to bring visitors to this raised small cottage clad with random-width cypress. Large overhangs of the hipped roof provide shade and protection for the openings that wrap the square plan. Built-in seating below the full-width, operable ribbon windows faces the interior central core of fireplace, kitchen, and more secluded bath. Butted glass at the corners extends the connection to the exterior while interior ceramic mosaic floors and a copper-clad fireplace help maximize "the richness of the experience of the inhabitants."[15] *House Beautiful* published an article about the house titled: "Palatial Living in a One Room House."

As Robert McCarter states,

this sense of economy, of gaining the maximum benefits for the enrichment of the inhabitants' daily rituals, over the

lifetime of a building, from the smallest energy and material investment, has always been part of the best modern architecture—and an ethical imperative for Alfred Browning.[16]

This rigorous efficiency even extended to Parker's working methods as just one sheet of working drawings was prepared for the Ewing Residence.

Halfway around the world, Kiyonori Kikutake designed his own house in central Tokyo a few years after he received his architecture degree. Kikutake, who was of the seventeenth generation of landowning farmers in his family, was deeply connected to the fertile agricultural land of his upbringing. His work reconstructing Tokyo after World War II helped direct his future architectural investigations.[17] He learned about the adaptability of wood construction. He also wondered how one could plan for dismantling and reconstruction. He looked

Figure I.6 Sky House by Kiyonori Kikutake

at providing two types of architectural space: one that was permanent and one that will eventually need rebuilding. He applied his experiences and developing thoughts to the design of the Sky House in 1958.

The house sits on a concrete platform supported by four large concrete piers, lifting the house 20 feet in the air. The creation of this "artificial ground" provided safety and a substructure for his family. The concrete superstructure provides the framework upon which later additions, called "move-nets" and used as bedrooms for his children, were hung. The main living room is a place where multiple functions or activities can take place. The central space, a "16 tatami mat" room, is the same size as his family house in his hometown of Kurume. A layer of sliding shutters and another layer of sliding glass panels define a balcony that wraps the perimeter of the house, allowing occupants to vary the relationship to the weather and exterior conditions. In order to facilitate future additions or changes, the kitchen and bathroom mechanical areas project into this zone between the sliding glass and the wood shutters. Kikutake, a leader in the Metabolism movement, whose conference brought American architect Louis Kahn all the way to Tokyo in 1960, describes three principles of architecture as: essence,

substance, and phenomenon.[18] The Sky House became the center of that movement as well as the center for his family.

Similar experimentation can be seen in the work of Albert Frey. Frey was born in Switzerland and worked, for a period, for Le Corbusier on the design of Villa Savoye. Frey arrived in Palm Springs, California in 1934 and built several houses for himself, as well as a wide range of buildings for his clients. Frey balanced modern architectural vocabulary with the regional forms of the hot, arid desert. His book *In Search of a Living Architecture*, published in 1939, documents his fascination with modern technology and the undeniably powerful landscape he was working within. Frey encouraged "culturally sensitive people" to see the artistic possibilities in the modern technologies often developed by engineers and practical concerns.[19] Frey's earlier collaboration with Lawrence Kocher on the Aluminaire House and experiments with treated canvas walls reflect his long-standing interest in experimenting with industrial materials.

In this second of the three houses he built in Palm Springs, Frey centered the design of the house around an existing stone boulder on-site. The rock protrudes into the main living

Figure I.7 Frey House II by Albert Frey

space, forcing a dynamic geometry on an otherwise simple orthogonal room. The house both "sits within and is passive and overpowered by the rock outcropping of the mountainside upon which it has been situated."[20] Frey designed a modern steel frame and glass-walled building that opens to the pool and the views to the south. All utility and support functions, including the bath, kitchen, and laundry, are placed on the west side of the simple rectangular plan, buffering the living space from the hot afternoon sun and allowing it to feel like a glass pavilion on three sides. A thin metal roof extends like a knife to intercept the sun overhead. Access to the house is gained from a switchback exterior staircase that leads from the carport, placed confidently below the pool. This house, built in 1963, "encapsulates all of Frey's ideas about nature and the man-made, about the poetic beauty of living a life intimately connected to the human scale."[21]

Other dwellings influence architectural practice due to their proximity to life in time and space. The list of work influencing contemporary practice in Houston, Texas is long and expansive. I will concentrate on only my two earliest personal influences.[22]

Joe and Julia Mashburn designed the Long Skinny House With a Kink in It on a six-acre property near College Station, Texas when Joe was teaching at Texas A&M University. The project, now famously owned by their long-time friend Lyle Lovett, caused quite a stir when it was built in 1985. The house, designed and built during the height of postmodernism, uses traditional vernacular forms and materials to create a modest regional response to climate and place. The corrugated metal-clad box twists in the middle to avoid existing trees on the site. This kink—a screened-in porch—serves to unite and separate the sleeping and living functions in this train-shaped house which reflects Joe's long-standing interest in trailers, trains, and automobiles. In 1972, when he was studying architecture at the University of Houston,[23] he utilized an Airstream trailer to make an almost instant addition to a small 700-square-foot house he owned.

Figure I.8 Long Skinny House With a Kink in It by Joe and Julia Mashburn

Casa Jimenez, designed by Carlos Jimenez, created new architectural lore when it was completed in 1984 in Houston. The urban myth that Carlos Jimenez had paid for its construction with credit cards easily expanded the story and dated it as being both truly modern and definitely of its place. The simple cube of living space, balanced by the studio in back, appeared to my designer mind to be perfectly situated. Perhaps the reduced lines and geometry fed the almost dreamlike quality of the minimalist work, whose image was larger than its square footage. Through this work, Jimenez introduced a new generation of architects to Luis Barragán and an appreciation of modesty in architecture. His self-described "search for a language of simplicity and clarity"[24] continues to resonate quietly in the fast and furious space of the "energy city."

Jimenez focuses on the larger context of Houston: he particularizes its light quality, local construction strategies, the extensive tree canopy, and the color of its sky at sunset. The original house, both buried and revealed in the current structure, expanded six times in twenty years, often contradicts itself. It is located at the front of the composition of buildings yet is no longer the entrance. The original house has stayed stationary while all movement has happened behind

Figure I.9 Casa Jimenez by Carlos Jimenez

it, and yet it remains the space in which Jimenez still designs, thinks, talks, and dwells in architecture.

The twenty projects presented in this book owe much to the above-mentioned examples and to the long lineage of architects whose small-focused investigations, due to their scale, allow us time to slow down and absorb a quiet architecture.

Just as architecture changes, the notion of home is also changing, though as noted by Krisch and Jocher, "our homes change surprisingly slowly by comparison to societal, economic, and cultural change."[25] Family structure is changing. The percentage of US households consisting of a married couple with children was just 20 percent in 2010, down from 44 percent in 1960.[26] New models of cohabitation, revival of the medieval integration of work and habitation, and a less formal division between private and public spaces provide the opportunity to take another look at contemporary dwellings. The small dwelling can be seen as more than a compromise between one's dream home and actual buying power. It can also offer clear lessons about architecture.

Each of these twenty buildings are 1,000 square feet or less. Some are truly full-time houses, yet some are singular spaces for limited duration and activities. Each is instructive for how we might dwell in the world. These shelters are simple. They are often—though not always—modest in cost. They are careful in their energy use and particular about how they sit on the land. The "land" in this case can range from a sloping site in rural Colorado to a flat site with nearby neighbors, or even the rooftop of a large warehouse.

Ideas of dwelling and sense of shelter within these twenty projects are focused and intensified. These are not miniature large houses—their design embodies the modest scale of the enclosure. As noted by the Swiss architect Gustavo Gili Galfetti:

> Small family houses, the product of a private commission, constitute one of the few fields of privileged experimentation to observe at close quarters how domestic dreams of their occupants and the creative capacity of their architects combine to achieve an architecture which acts as a nexus between man and nature.[27]

Small dwellings usually include a highly prioritized program, reflect a warm relationship between the client and the architect, are designed and built quickly (and therefore provide feedback quickly), and usually have limited administration or financial issues to deal with. These are often "intimate, secluded, and protective space[s],"[28] full of ingenuity, and flexible in their use, while offering a degree of protection. Smaller dwellings provide a space that is more capable of being protected; "it is roughly true that the smaller the domain to be controlled, the more controllable it is."[29] These are not portable shelters, like clothes or cars. Most do not prioritize or even recognize the car; the dwellings shown here have entrances for people, not for automobiles.

Small does not always equate with simplicity, yet a simplified program or scope "allows a more involved architectural investigation."[30] Even when designing his own house, in

Orinda, California in 1962, in which he incorporated many of his ideas of the temple and the sign in the small structure, Charles Moore also "rigorously excluded from his list of requirements all of those things that were not demonstrably necessary,"[31] suggesting that even in a small house it is difficult to determine what is necessary.

Moore also wrote, in his book *In Place of Houses*, that we can think about houses in terms of the arrangement of space, light, focus, and outlook in the various rooms. Beyond a similarity of scale, the small, efficient structures included in this book clearly reveal a particular attitude towards materiality, light, enclosure, and accommodation that speaks directly to efficiency.

The resolution of complex relationships are not typically required when designing a dwelling unit that is less than 1,000 square feet. Building systems are often simplified or even eliminated while just the architectural elements remain. The exterior skin—the assembly that regulates the relationship to the external environment and determines how light is allowed to enter the space—can be thick or thin, porous or punctured. The skin wraps around a volume of space that might be compressed, elongated, extended, horizontal, vertical, or raised. Within the volume, the spaces can be fixed or flexible. Relationships between public and private activities can be defined or blurred. Architects of small dwellings get to focus on only these essential architectural issues.

The skin's thickness and porosity are determined in part by the material and assemblage systems. As Peter Zumthor reminds us "materials in architecture can be made to shine and vibrate" and "their tangibility, smell, acoustic qualities are merely elements of the language that we are obliged to use."[32] Materials on interior surfaces reflect light, and these surfaces can heighten the contrast between light and dark. Materials determine more than the visual character of the building. "The skin reads the texture, weight, density and temperature of matter."[33] Often, a small house has a very specific material palette. Using fewer materials can quiet the space. Architects may challenge a limited palette by using one material in several ways. Materials also have an acoustic quality, and it is often only in our dwellings that we have the opportunity to slow down enough to actually listen to the space around us.

Light is brought into the space through the exterior walls and roof. Introducing light from multiple directions can make a smaller space feel more expansive and connected to the exterior. In smaller houses, light is allowed inside using particular methods and strategies that are simply easier to manage when there are fewer openings in a more compact building. "Light is of decisive importance in experiencing architecture."[34] Steen Eiler Rasmussen, the twentieth-century Danish architect and planner, also reminds us "the quantity of light is not nearly as important as its quality."[35] For human comfort, light should be balanced or controllable and should come from multiple directions. This allows the light to animate the space across the play of time over the course of a day or season. Because different material surfaces will reflect or absorb light in a variety of ways, the architect can manipulate light as a material quality: it can be "soft, sharp, pellucid (admitting maximum passage of light without diffusion or distortion), crystalline."[36]

The apertures in the buildings' skins determine the various aspects of the world they will admit; beyond allowing light to penetrate into the building, apertures also admit breeze, sound, and views. Each of these is also influenced by the relative orientation of the volume. Le Corbusier famously wrote about Adolf Loos describing a more limited function of a window: "A friend once said to me, 'No intelligent man ever looks out of his window; his window is made of ground glass; its only function is to let in light, not to look out of.'"[37]

Many people believe that "natural light has all of the moods of the time of day, the seasons of the year, (which) year for year and day for day are different from the day preceding,"[38] and "no space, architecturally, is a space unless it has natural light."[39] Others believe that darkness should also be designed. Just as a variety of light levels make for a more interesting space, a variation of shadows and places where darkness can gather

is equally important. Tanizaki argues for a layering of "heavy shadows against light shadows"[40] in spaces.

The enclosure system, including the wall assemblage and its light-admitting apertures, also defines space and its relationship to the landscape beyond. Often, smaller houses are connected to the exterior in particular ways in order to increase the spatial sequence. In describing one of his designs, Charles Moore wrote "the distinction between indoors and out is at once sharp and manipulable."[41] In a small building, there is often only one door for entry, and that moment of arrival, opening, and closing can be a heightened and expanded experience.

Prioritizing the issues and activities to be accommodated allows the building to be more finely tuned to its users and surroundings. This becomes even more important in a smaller project "where every square inch counts."[42]

> The experience of home is structured by distinct activities—cooking, eating, socializing, reading, storing, sleeping, intimate acts—not by visual elements. A building is encountered; it is approached, confronted, related to one's body, moved through, and utilized as a condition for other things. Architecture initiates, directs and organizes behavior and movement.[43]

Smaller dwellings must be fitted more specifically to the user and use than is required in a larger home. While rooms "are the empty stages for human activity,"[44] a successful dwelling might be more like a "close fitting little house"[45] and the architecture must negotiate between the two.

Juhani Pallasmaa argues for an architecture that is less visually dominated and that architecture depends upon the body to shape space.[46] The buildings in the following chapters, while visually beautiful, were designed as places to dwell completely and specifically. Each small building negotiates between various qualities: quiet and loud, light and dark, clarity and cloudiness, heavy and light, solid and porous, tall and low, and dream and reason. The elegance of each solution is exhibited in the simplicity, order, and care in the crafting of the spaces. These projects are more than merely small. Their limited scope simply allows for more clarity as we study the strength of the ideas expressed.

Although the houses included in this book have been designed by architects, and built by contractors for specific clients, a small home does give the impression of independence and self-reliance. Tom Peters argues, in his essay "An American Culture of Construction," that light timber framing (now more commonly referred to as platform framing) is uniquely related to a democratic political system and allows for individuals to modify (or build) their own houses due to the simplicity and redundancy of the framing system.[47] A house of less than 1,000 square feet is a size we each could imagine actually building ourselves. Yet, as demonstrated by Edward Cline and Buster Keaton's film *One Week*, not every homeowner should attempt to build their own dwelling.

Architectural education prepared Alex Melamed to build his own house. Melamed became fascinated with the tiny house movement and its focus on resource conservation. He designed the Walnut House for himself, his wife, and their cat in a small Ohio town. The house is merely 300 square feet and includes a sleeping loft. After its completion, Melamed wondered how a voluntary simplicity might alter how they lived. He and his wife have found it is not as difficult as their friends and family imagined. They live in a walkable community; the ability to easily walk to the nearby neighborhood library or local coffee shop makes them feel part of a larger community and greatly expands their "living" space. They use the house's common space for most activities, and they have invested in comfortable multifunctional furniture (in fact, they admit the pullout sofa is the most comfortable bed in the house) and reduced or eliminated most of the items associated with hobbies. This simplification also necessitates tidying up after each activity before switching to the next. The only problem so far arises if they both try to use the desk at the same time. Cooking is very important to the couple and they

did not compromise on the space allocated to their "live-in" kitchen. They can host a dinner party for six, using their folding chairs and an extra leaf for the table, and now enjoy more kitchen counter space than in their previous apartment.

Often, small is not the starting point, but is arrived at due to budget constraints. Bryn Davidson learned a lot when he and his wife downsized their home and bought what was, at that time, the cheapest house for sale in Vancouver. He says:

> We had a strong belief that the amount of space that was "necessary" was completely arbitrary, and that—with a substantial redesign—we could create something not just livable, but very comfortable. We bought the condo (we dubbed it "the pod") and took it on as an experiment in small footprint living; an experiment in making 360 square feet comfortable for a couple.[48]

They happily lived in the small house for three years, often hosting dinner parties for ten. In late 2008, the loss of projects due to the recession allowed Davidson and his business partner Mat Turner to combine their interests in sustainability and small housing just as Vancouver was adopting the Laneway Housing program. Vancouver provides a good fit for building smaller infill houses on residential lots due to the lack of vacant land and very high real estate costs. Davidson and Turner's company, Lanefab, now designs and builds contemporary custom infill and laneway projects. While small houses are expensive to build on a per-square-foot basis, many young couples are finding that laneway housing can be less expensive that a condominium if their family already owns the land. Lanefab is now beginning a partnership with a company in Australia to build similar laneway houses in Melbourne.

Smaller dwellings also lend themselves to considering prefabrication since size and highway shipping dimensions are a concern for prefabricated structures. Prefabrication requires small units for ease of movement and are a recent response to changing family size, economies, and the increasing density of cities. It can offer an alternative to small dwellings designed by architects for specific clients. Alchemy Architects of Minnesota has developed the weeHouse for similar situations and has built over thirty units around the country. Lake/Flato Architects have developed the Porch House, a set of modular rooms that can stand alone as a single unit or be combined. Greg Kearly with Washington DC's Inscape Modular is beginning to market a small 650-square-foot home with all components of the house—closets, bed, desk, storage, and cabinets—built-in to maximize space. Houston architect Brett Zamore offers kit homes of just 400 square feet and up to 1,000 square feet, two of which have been built. International design firm LOT-EK, founded in 1993, has been interested in using man-made objects. Its Mobile Dwelling Unit, designed in 2003, is just 500 square feet and uses standard shipping containers and systems to allow dwellers to travel the globe with their home.

Marmol Radziner Prefab from Los Angeles offers several sizes of prefabricated homes. The Rincon series is just 660 square feet and, according to their website, can be "designed for use as a guesthouse, office, or vacation home. Each unit arrives complete with all finishes, appliances, fixtures and cabinets in place, providing an instant vacation retreat or solution."[49] The unit is 12 feet by 56 feet and includes the kitchen, living, bedroom with covered deck; recycled steel construction, concrete floors, SIP[50] panels, Heath tile, integrated ductless heating/cooling, high-performance glazing, extensive operable glass, full privacy shades, Caesarstone countertops, and full walnut cabinetry. One unit of this size has been built and was delivered to a site in Venice, California. While the cost varies based on a number of factors—such as location and property conditions—it is possible that prefab construction costs about the same as comparable quality site-built construction.

Small-scale dwellings also match up nicely with university design-build projects. A student team can realistically build a minimal scope structure in a summer or a semester. The Rice Building Workshop, run by architects Danny Samuels and Nonya Grenader, designed and built the 500-square-foot Extra-Small House for $25,000 in the Third Ward of Houston. The house is a modern interpretation of the "shotgun houses"

that still exist in this neighborhood just east of downtown. The simple gabled structure has one long west wall that is thickened to provide places for storage and equipment. This thicker wall also helps insulate the interior from the hot Texas afternoon sun. A bathroom core, clad in translucent polycarbonate, brings light into the volume and separates the larger space from a smaller space. Each space can be used for varying activities and is served by porches on both gable ends.

In 2011, Rick Sommerfeld's University of Colorado design-build program, Colorado Building Workshop, teamed up with DesignBuildBLUFF at the University of Utah. The CU-Denver students designed and built a 745-square-foot house for a teacher with a large collection of books and a great interest in the bugs and plant life of the desert climate. The resulting Nakai Residence forms a courtyard with three existing houses, each to be occupied by family members when they visit the Navajo Nation in the southeast Utah desert. The metal shed roof twists to open up to the views of the Navajo mountain that are part of the owner's childhood history and slopes down in the private areas of the house. A 6 foot by 6 foot window box projects from the face of the building and focuses on a tree, recalling the former orchard that stood on this land. The exterior is clad in spandrel glass that was donated—after it was mis-ordered for an office building. Above 8 feet, the exterior cladding is "shou-sugi-ban" which is burnt cedar siding. Burning the wood naturally seals it, making it resistant to insects and fire. A 50-foot-long bookcase on the interior divides one large room for painting, dining, living, and dancing from the bedroom nook, bathroom, storage, and kitchen.

In 2002, the US Department of Energy started the Solar Decathlon, a design competition, now held every other year, for multidisciplinary university student-and-faculty teams to design small, energy-efficient dwellings. The house size is limited to 600 to 1,000 square feet. The houses are then subjectively and objectively evaluated. Many qualities of the design, including the architectural narrative, engineering, cost, and even the ease of hosting dinner parties, are evaluated by a juried team. Energy use, indoor temperature and humidity,

FLOOR PLAN
1 entry
2 kitchen
3 bathroom
4 living

Figure I.10 Extra-Small House floor plan

and water use are measured or monitored. The dwellings are typically prefabricated at each university and then transported to Washington DC for completion, testing, and the eight-day competition and public exhibit event. The houses often return to their host institution for further research, testing of systems, and demonstrations after the competition. Past Solar Decathalon houses are distributed across the US, Europe, and Asia, and one is now even in New Zealand.[51]

There are many inspiring examples of small houses in Europe, Asia, and South America. In North America, where the majority of households live in detached dwellings, architects continue to accept commissions for smaller projects, regardless of the challenges. In Los Angeles, the BIG & small House by Anonymous is a free-plan arrangement within a parallelogram volume. A double-height living space takes up the majority of the volume with a sleeping loft perched over a bathroom tucked into one corner. The Seattle office of Bohlin Cywinski Jackson is currently working on two small projects. One project, called the Bunkie, looks at providing elemental shelter where occupants can choose the privacy or communal nature of the sleeping space. Elliott + Associates Architects,

in Oklahoma City, is designing a 1,000-square-foot house of concrete, glass, and metal located near the Chinati Foundation property in Marfa, Texas. The project's materiality works well in the rough-and-tumble landscape of west Texas, and its courtyard allows a more complete integration of the land and interior.

A few homes included in this book are designed for use as a primary residence. There are significant differences between designing a primary house and designing a weekend or single-purpose building. Weekend houses allow for more flexibility, require less space for the storage of items, and more variation is allowed in terms of thermal comfort. People are willing to "try something on" in a weekend or vacation home that they might not allow in their permanent houses and give architects the "freedom to interpret people's life-styles in the experimental realm of vacation living."[52] Secondary dwellings often need to accommodate entertaining and guests but not necessarily the owner's prized collections or closets full of clothes.

Secondary dwellings often lend themselves to a more adaptable program as people are not always sure how they will use the space, unlike a primary dwelling where they usually have an idea on how they will live in the spaces.[53] Architect Julie Eizenberg[54] thinks we no longer know what is functionally optimal in a home. Often clients are concerned with making sure kids are sleeping close to parents. While this works when kids are young, eventually no one wants to be that close to each other anymore. Clients and architects should think ten years out and envision daily life happening in a variety of places.

Architects will often alter their schedules and design processes when designing a smaller dwelling unit. The process should be streamlined and efficient. Often, the method of construction—assembly systems, materials, and exactly who will agree to build such a small project—needs to be thought out in advance. Rarely does the architect's fee cover all the work that the architect must do in a smaller-scope project. Per-foot construction costs do not make much sense in a small project,

Figure I.11 Extra-Small House by Rice Building Workshop

and architect's fees in relationship to construction costs are equally misaligned. In addition, as noted by architect Ted Flato, "you had better really like the client and the project because you will not make a lot of money on a small house."[55] Architect Sebastian Schmaling agrees: "You can't really bill every hour that you work on a small house because there is a limit to what a client will pay. This is why fewer smaller projects are designed by architects."[56] John Grable, whose work is also included in this book, admits that sometimes the big projects pay for the little ones, yet the small projects advance the big ideas.

Not only did the architects interviewed for this book like their clients, they really enjoyed working on the projects. These small-scale projects progress without a difficult school board to work with or complicated code issues to resolve. The architects remember fondly their time spent working on these projects and the opportunity to engage once again with only the most primary issues of architecture: enclosure, materials, light, and accommodating the act of dwelling.

Notes

1   Charles Moore, "Foreword," in *In Praise of Shadows*, Junichiro Tanizaki (Connecticut: Leete's Island Books, 1977).

2   Banister Fletcher, *A History of Architecture on the Comparative Method* (London: B. T. Batsford, 1924, 7th edition) p. 1.

3   Junichiro Tanizaki, *In Praise of Shadows* (Connecticut: Leete's Island Books, 1977), p. 17.

4   Roderick Kemsley and Christopher Platt, *Dwelling with Architecture* (Virginia: Routledge, 2012), p. 83.

5   Bob Ransford, email correspondence with author, January 2014.

6   Steven Holl, *Pamphlet Architecture 9: Rural and Urban House Types in North America* (New York: Princeton Architectural Press, 1982).

7   Rudiger Krisch and Thomas Jocher, "The Image of the House," in *Single Family Houses: Concepts, Planning, and Construction*, Christian Schittich and Thomas Jocher (eds) (Boston: Birkhauser, 2000, pp. 28–41), p. 37.

8   Kemsley and Platt, p. 117.

Figure I.13 Nakai Residence by Colorado Building Workshop

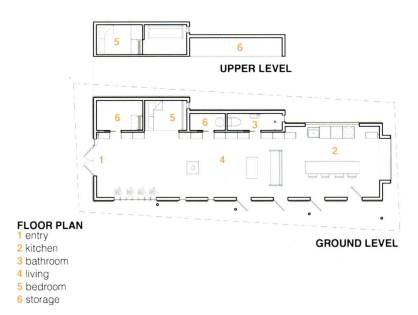

FLOOR PLAN
1 entry
2 kitchen
3 bathroom
4 living
5 bedroom
6 storage

Figure I.12 Nakai Residence floor plan

9 Filippo Alison, *Le Corbusier: Interior of the Cabanon* (Milão, Cassina, 2006), p. 12.

10 Cited in Alison, p. 48.

11 Holl, Steven. *Pamphlet Architecture 9: Rural & Urban House Types in North America.* (New York, 1982), p. 6. Steven Holl writes about how early rural and urban houses display a straightforwardness of construction clarity – qualities that are also shared with Le Corbusier's cabanon.

12 Tim Benton, "Historic Houses: Le Corbusier's Cabanon," *Architectural Digest 44*, December 1987, pp. 146–51, quotation on p. 147. Le Corbusier did die near his *cabanon*. He had a heart attack while swimming nearby.

13 Oscar Riera Oejda, ed., *Casas Internacional: Carlos Jimenez* (Hong Kong: Klickowski Publisher, 1996), p. 84.

14 Randolph C. Henning, *The Architecture of Alfred Browning Parker: Miami's Maverick Modernist,* with a foreword by Robert McCarter (2011 Gainesville, FL: University Press of Florida, pp. ix–xv), pp. ix–x.

15 Henning, pp. xiv–xv.

16 Henning, p. xv.

17 Kiyonori Kikutake, *Kiyonori Kikutake: From Tradition to Utopia* (Milan: l'Arca Edizione, 1997).

18 Westcott, James. "Obit: Kiyonori Kikutake, 1928–2011. James Westcott Reflects on the Life and Work of a Leader of the Metabolist Movement," *The Architect's Newspaper,* February 15, 2012. http://archpaper.com/news/articles.asp?id=5888#.U-ybp1aprwl

19 Albert Frey, *In Search of a Living Architecture* (New York: Architectural Book Publishing Co., Inc., 1939), p. 35.

20 Joseph Rosa, *Albert Frey, Architect,* with a foreword by David Gebhard (New York: Rizzoli, 1990), p. xi.

21 Nicolai Ouroussoff, "Albert Frey, Modernist Architect Dies," *Los Angeles Times,* November 17, 1998. http://articles.latimes.com

22 Practicing architecture in Houston involves being part of a community of energetic and talented architects. We are influenced by what is built around us. John Zemanek's three houses, each getting smaller and with changing focuses, encourage a continual refinement of ideas. Victor Lundy's exquisitely executed renovation of an adobe house in Marfa, Texas shelters occupants under a wood-lined tent roof and is a natural extension of his work in Sarasota, Florida. The work of other contemporary architects including Natalye Appel, Val Glitsch, Nonya Grenader, Karen Lantz, Carrie Glassman Shoemake, and the late William Stern continue to shape this city and current architectural practice.

23 I was a student at Texas A&M University when the Long Skinny House With a Kink in It was built. Later, I designed a house for my parents and named it A Very Long Skinny House in reference to the influence of the Mashburns' house on my own work. Joe Mashburn later served as Dean at the University of Houston from 1998 until 2010, where he continues to teach part-time.

24 Oejda, p. 68.

25 Rudiger Krisch and Thomas Jocher, "The Image of the House," in *Single Family Houses: Concepts, Planning, and Construction,* Christian Schittich and Thomas Jocher (eds) (Boston: Birkhauser, 2000, pp. 28–43), p. 29.

26 According to the US census, the average size of a new house in 1973 was 1,660 square feet and in 2010 it was 2,443 square feet (an increase of 47 percent)—US Census Bureau. www.census.gov

27 Gustavo Gili Galfetti, *Casas Refugio: Private Retreats* (Barcelona: Editorial Gustavo Gili, 1999), p. 8.

28 Galfetti, p. 13.

29 Serge Chermayeff and Christopher Alexander, *Community and Privacy: Toward a New Architecture of Humanism* (New York: Doubleday, 1963), p. 143.

30 Kemsley and Platt, p. 11.

31 Charles Moore, Gerard Allen, and Donlyn Lyndon, *The Place of Houses* (Los Angeles: Holt, University of California Press, 2000), p. 59.

32 Peter Zumthor, *Thinking Architecture* (Birkhauser, 1998), p. 10.

33 Juhani Pallasmaa, *The Eyes of the Skin: Architecture and the Senses* (West Sussex: John Wiley & Sons, 2005), p. 56.

34 Steen Eiler Rasmussen, "Daylight in Architecture," in *Experiencing Architecture* (Boston: MIT Press, 1991, pp. 186–223), p. 187.

35 Rasmussen, p. 189.

36 Moore, Allen, and Lyndon, p. 97.

37 Le Corbusier, *The City of Tomorrow and its Planning* (New York: Dover Publications, Inc., 1987), pp. 184–6.

38 Louis Kahn, *Light is the Theme* (Fort Worth: Kimball Art Foundation, 2002), p. 18.

39 Kahn, p. 15.

40 Tanizaki, p. 18.

41 Moore, Allen, and Lyndon, p. 61. A series of sliding panels, the Budge House of 1966, allows the interior space to connect to the forest.

42 Nonya Grenader, interview with author. Houston, Texas. August 2012.

43 Pallasmaa, p. 63.

44 Moore, Allen, and Lyndon, p. 67.

45 Moore, Allen, and Lyndon, p. 237.

46 Pallasmaa, p. 56.

47 Tom Peters, "An American Culture of Construction," *Perspecta* 25, 1989, pp. 142–61.

48 Bryn Davidson, email messages and phone interview with author. January 2014.

49 Marmol Radziner, "Rincon Series." www.marmolradzinerprefab.com/products/rincon/

50 SIP stands for structurally insulated panels.

51 I spent the night in the BeauSoleil, a 2009 Solar Decathalon entry, after giving a talk at the University of Louisiana at Lafayette. The BeauSoleil won the People's Choice Award and is open to the public for visits.

52 Moore, Allen, and Lyndon, p. viii.

53 John Grable, phone interview with author. February 2014.

54 Julie Eizenberg, interview with author. Los Angeles. January 2014.

55 Ted Flato, interview with author. San Antonio. December 2013.

56 Sebastian Schmaling, phone interview with author. August 2013.

Timeline

1949 **Glass House**
Phillip Johnson

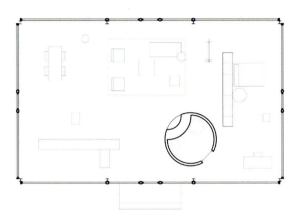

1949 **Cocoon House**
Paul Rudolph

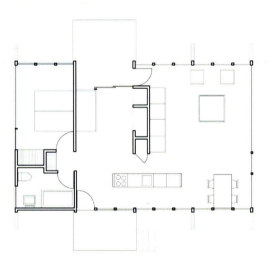

1951 **Farnsworth House**
Mies van der Rohe

Cabanon 1952
Le Corbusier

Ewing Residence 1955
Alfred Browning Parker

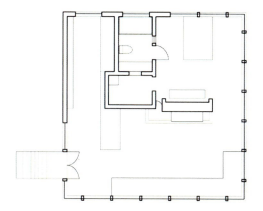

Sky House 1958
Kiyonori Kikutake

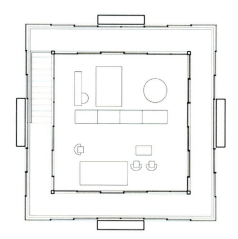

1958 **Frey House II**
Albert Frey

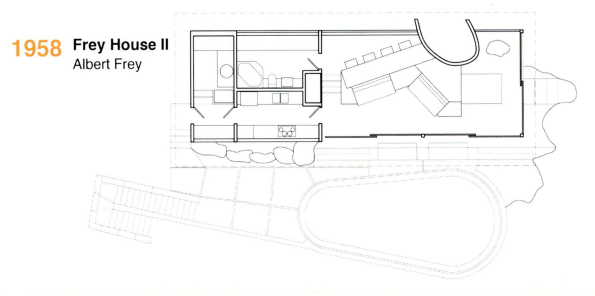

1974 **Crane Island Cabin**
Wendel Lovett

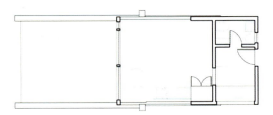

1984 **Casa Jimenez**
Carlos Jimenez

Long Skinny House 1985
with a Kink in It
Joe and Julia Mashburn

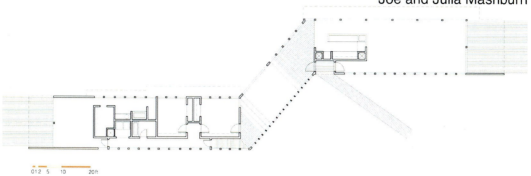

0 1 2 5   10   20 ft

Kemper Cabin 1992
Suyama Peterson
Deguchi

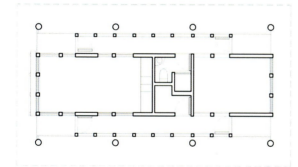

Hill Country Jacal 1997
Lake/Flato

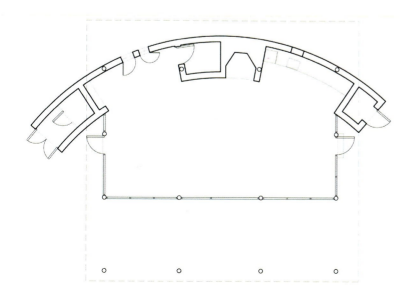

2000 **Keenan Tower House**
Marlon Blackwell Architect

2003 **Scholar's Library**
GLUCK +

2004 **Ravine Guest House**
Shim-Sutcliffe

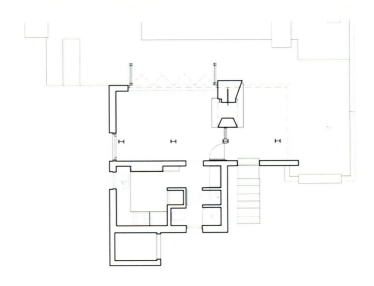

Craven Road Studio 2006
Shim-Sutcliffe

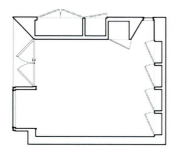

Envelope House 2006
Bohlin Cywinski Jackson

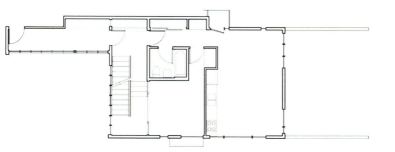

Marfa 10x10 2007
Candid Rogers Studio

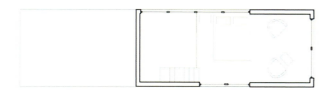

2007 **Writer's Studio**
Cooper Joseph Studio

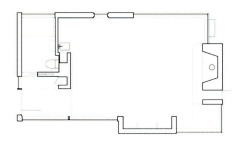

2007 **Blossom Street House**
Nonya Grenader

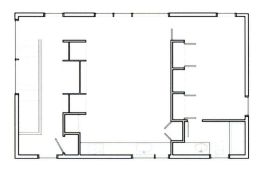

2008 **Watershed**
FLOAT

Williams Cabin 2008
Atkinson Architecture

Pool House 2009
Koning Eizenberg

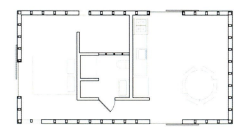

Roland Cabin 2009
David Salmela

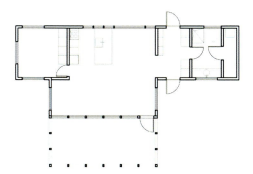

2010 False Bay Writer's Cabin
Olson Kundig Architects

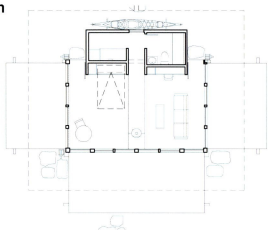

2010 Sky Ranch
The Miller Hull Partnership

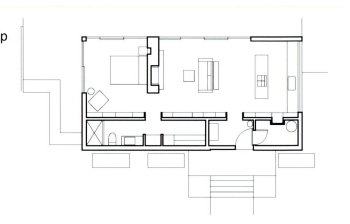

2010 Small House in an Olive Grove
Cooper Joseph Studio

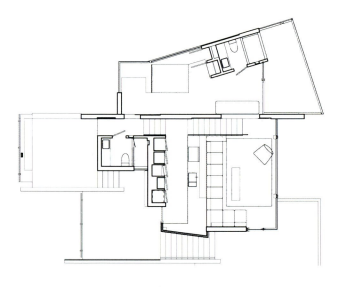

Music Box 2012
John Grable Architects, Inc.

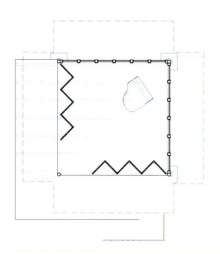

Stacked Cabin 2012
Johnsen Schmaling Architects

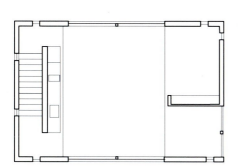

Nested House 2014
LOJO Architecture

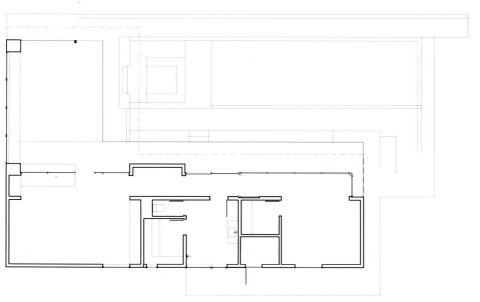

Variant ONE
Porous Dwellings

These buildings are designed to be used for a limited time or limited activities. They are truly connected to their environment, the climate, and nature. Porous structures may closely resemble camping structures yet are highly tuned to a specific site or activity.

1

Watershed

FLOAT

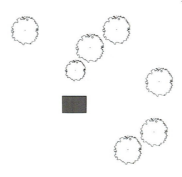

Watershed
FLOAT

Wren, Oregon   44.6°N, 123.4°W   2008

70 SF

FLOOR PLAN
1 entry

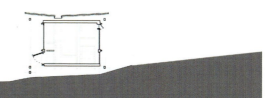

Figure 1.2 Watershed view from the field

This shed, not quite a house, provides a serene yet porous space in which to dwell and focus on nature. The client asked for a place to write that provided maximum views and light in the rainy Pacific Northwest climate while truly connecting to the hydrology of the place. Moore edited the views and curated the light so they no longer felt infinite. To make the rain more visible, the thin roof gently slopes towards a trough that directs the water to a shallow elongated metal basin that one must step across to enter the shelter.

Moore is experimental in her use of materials; she looks for new applications for often overlooked materials. This project demonstrates a clear logic to the material selections and their location in the overall assembly. Concrete, coded as the most permanent material, provides the minimal footings for the foundation. Steel, a semipermanent material, is used as the exterior frame. One enters the zone of the steel frame first, then the thin enclosure system. Western red cedar wood cladding, classified as nonpermanent, slides in between the steel frame. Glass panels allow the light into the space and provide views to the nature beyond. A thin polycarbonate roof hovers over the structure, diffusing light while amplifying

the sound of rain. All materials, except for the steel frame, were hand-carried to the site. The building connects to the ground in a delicate way in order to not undermine the site's wildness. This light landing on the earth is only possible in a transient dwelling where the implications of long-term human habitation do not require attention.

This structure, designed to have a minimal impact on the land, is also designed to be demountable. Very few screws or attachments hold everything together—the ephemeral quality of the space is provided by this loose fit of components. The tongue-and-groove cedar cladding panels slide into a dado—a slot reveal—and can easily slide out in order to be carried away and return this piece of the Willamette Valley to the way it was found.

FLOAT Architectural Research and Design is a small architectural practice in Eugene, Oregon, started by Erin Moore. Moore's small projects, informed by her habitation research, offer a different relationship between client and architect than traditional architectural practice. Her projects are more like a hand-tailored piece of clothing. Her design

Figure 1.3 Watershed view from the writing desk

services cannot be measured against more standard architectural services. She spends a great amount of time getting to know the client in order to determine what is absolutely essential to them and to the project. Moore unwillingly spent much of her childhood camping, with her biologist father and nature-writer mother, and built forts in order to find comfort in the outdoors. She will now often start her projects with nothing, and then, as if camping, determine what is needed. She might start with something to act as an umbrella to provide shelter from the rain and then add something else to provide shade, and so on. She has used masking tape and sticks to make physical mock-ups or visited equivalent structures to know what the space feels like and to get an exact fit. The specific position in the landscape is as important as size or dimension. Oftentimes, she will put a client on a ladder, mimicking the potential experience, while videotaping the entire action for future study and refinement.

OPPOSITE TOP
Figure 1.4 Watershed back elevation

OPPOSITE BELOW
Figure 1.5 Watershed large looking glass window faces field

2

Music Box

John Grable Architects, Inc.

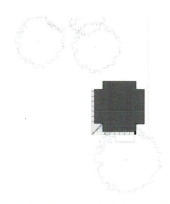

Music Box
John Grable Architects, Inc.

Sisterdale, Texas   30.0°N, 98.7°W   2012

400 SF

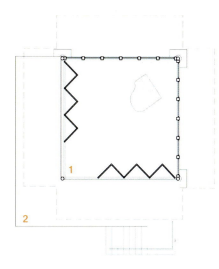

FLOOR PLAN
1 entry
2 deck

Figure 2.2 Music Box exterior view

This single room, built for music and yoga, sits under the shade of broad-branched live oak trees near a tributary to the Guadalupe River in a small agricultural community in Central Texas. The structure is lifted up out of the floodplain to float above the land and focuses on the limestone-faced waterfall in the cypress-lined creek bank just 100 yards away. For architect John Grable, each project starts by addressing the building program and budget constraints early in order to determine what is essential to the project, sometimes throwing out the so-called "givens" along the way. Balancing early decisions, such as the budget and scope, while still being able to listen to the final solution is akin to setting the values early in the building design process and then letting go after "good parenting."[1]

In this project, the architect and client prioritized providing shelter and conditioned space for the piano. Focusing on providing the best acoustic environment for the grand piano led to the final form of the building. Sheltered by a large lightweight roof, two wood-faced walls direct views and, more importantly, sound through the two open walls. A wood exterior deck connects the interior to the exterior.

The lightweight space is lifted off the ground by a welded steel frame of reclaimed oil field pipe. Welding the connections, rather than using mechanical fasteners, allows the structure to be stiffer and use less material while also achieving the desired lightness in both the floor and roof. A structural plywood deck, one and one-eighth inches thick, provides a solid substrate for the roof and two-inch-thick cypress planks are used for the floor. The increased depth of these solid planes allows the steel framing below to be spaced further apart. In order to limit the size of the primary structure, the secondary structure needed to be effectively distributed. Grable explained it was "like working a calculus problem"[2] and that often "the road to simplicity is a complicated path."[3] The use of reclaimed oil field pipe for the structural frame also provides a connection to the client's oil field history.

This Music Box is built on a ranch owned by five generations of oil field workers. The client requested a material palette shaped by the family history and serving as a reminder of their work ethic. Most surfaces are faced, both inside and outside, and on walls and floors, by reclaimed sinker cypress planks. Sinker cypress refers to wood from dense, slow-growing, first-growth cypress trees, felled in the early 1900s. Large logs were floated down waterways on large mats to transport them to the mills. Some logs were lost during transportation, became waterlogged and sank to the bottom of waterways, and have recently been recovered. This first-growth cypress has much tighter grain patterns and is much denser than second-growth trees. The horizontal cladding, installed with alternating bands of varying grain color and figure pattern, creates images reminiscent of the earth's strata in a boring log. This dense solid-grained wood also helps deflect and direct sound to the open doors. One wood wall is fitted with custom wall plates for the client's yoga practice.

The two open sides are fitted with a custom folding door system. The architects first investigated many preexisting systems but could not find one that opened in all directions, giving the user complete freedom in determining the porosity of the structure. The solution required patience and collaboration between the client, contractor, and craftsman. The doors can be opened at any location and each panel can swing in or out. The two walls of glass and steel doors act more like a curtain, providing a fluid and flexible surface that contrasts with the stability of the two fixed wood walls.

The hovering metal roof, with delicately thin overhangs, shelters the piano from any direct light. Instead, light reflects off the wood floor and the underside of the metal roof, and the warmth of the wood changes the color temperature of the light inside the space. Clerestory windows above the wood walls reduce glare and provide cross ventilation. The deck, almost the same size as the enclosed space, is cantilevered 8 feet from the five supporting piers, and extends the space into the canopy of the oak trees that surround the light and limber building.

John Grable Architects was established in San Antonio, Texas in 2004. Grable acknowledges that his office's procedures are the same, regardless of scale. Once the idea is developed, they work "like crazy" to get it detailed and built well. They start by balancing the aspects of architecture: site, program, materials, and detail. Often decisions are linked. In smaller projects, human dimensions need to be the measuring stick; at the intimate scale everything needs to be the exact right size. The margins are thinner and all elements are connected due to their proximity. In a small building there is "nowhere to hide."[4]

Figure 2.3 Music Box detail at exterior wall

Figure 2.4 Music Box interior wood walls and folding glass doors

Figure 2.5 Music Box view from piano looking towards landscape

Notes

1   John Grable, phone interview with author. February, 2014.
2   Ibid.
3   Ibid.
4   Ibid.

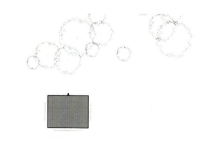

False Bay Writer's Cabin
Olson Kundig Architects

San Juan Island, Washington 48.5°N, 123.0°W   2010

500 SF

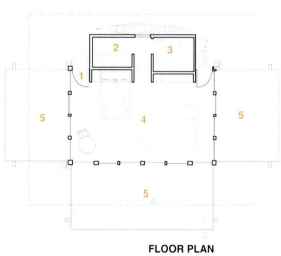

FLOOR PLAN
1 entry
2 kitchen
3 bathroom
4 big room
5 deck

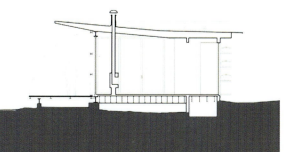

Figure 3.2 False Bay Writer's Cabin looking west from inside

The False Bay Writer's Cabin, located on the western edge of San Juan Island, is just 500 square feet, but the space feels expansive due to the visual connection to the landscape afforded by the transparent glass that wraps three sides of the house. "[Tom] Kundig's genius for closely packed and layered program"[1] is demonstrated here as well as in other small cabins such as the Chat-O Spapho, Tye River Cabin, and the Gulf Islands Cabin. The fragile enclosure is protected by wooden slat walls that, when in their lowered position, become an exterior deck. A hydraulic winch allows the "shutter decks" to protect the glass and act as the building's security system when fully raised. A rear core contains the bathroom and cooking area, faced with a thick layer of storage. This clear distinction between open space and core is reminiscent of Johnson's Glass House and Mies' Farnsworth House. All three share a careful study of the relationship between open frame and solid core.

In this case, the simple rectangular box is wrapped on three sides by 10-foot-tall glass panels, and its solid portions are clad in rusting steel. The whole volume is sheltered by the slightly inverted hip roof, surfaced with wood on the interior. The light wood floor is protected by the bisecting swath of raw steel plate that allows the heat-producing wood furnace to slide into its position relative to the exterior wall. The "shutter decks" further extend the space out to the landscape.

The clients, Maggie and Scotty Greene, lived in the "hut" (as they refer to it) while their main house was under construction. The term of endearment is a reference to its size and simplicity. The term also helped the team be more disciplined during the design phase. The Greenes remember calling a "time out" whenever someone said "we could add" or "we could put a," suggesting the addition of something that might increase the size of the building. The compact space was specifically sized to allow for many different activities. Four eight-person, round tables fit in the main space for dinner parties. A Murphy bed folds down from a wall to house any overnight guests. When the bed is flipped up to its storage position, the space is used as an exercise studio and as a writing studio—Maggie is currently working on a book project. While the kitchen area is compact, they learned that "you can do anything with a hot plate and a toaster oven."[2] Everything in the space transforms and has more than one function. The table is on wheels and

OPPOSITE TOP
Figure 3.3 False Bay Writer's Cabin looking south

OPPOSITE BELOW
Figure 3.4 False Bay Writer's Cabin entry near storage and Murphy bed

Figure 3.5 False Bay Writer's Cabin wood "shutter decks" halfway open

can be a desk or an outdoor dining table. Lightweight nesting coffee tables serve as nightstands when the Murphy bed is lowered. They purposefully decided not to have a television and have found that, in this space, there are no distractions. Even though the larger main house is now complete, the Greenes, who spend much of their time in Atlanta, always spend a few days in "the hut" each visit in order to reconnect with the site. They enjoyed working with Kundig and the entire creative process. They agree that: "A house by Tom Kundig is not a typical house; it is more than a machine for living, it is a machine for wondering."[3]

The clients and their vision of the project are most important to Olson Kundig Architects. The work of the Seattle-based firm is varied—it includes residences, museums, institutional, and commercial projects—but achieves great clarity, regardless of scale. The small cabins designed by Kundig distill shelter to its refined essentials. Kundig's interest in small houses—and in cabins in particular—has been reinforced by the rediscovery of a cabin from his youth. The cabin, with its slightly raised platform and butterfly roof, clearly articulated the notions of shelter, prospect, and refuge and captured the sense of joyful occupation that the architect seeks in his work.

Figure 3.6 False Bay Writer's Cabin night view

Notes

1   Daniel S. Friedman, "Man of Steel: Tom Kundig and the
    Architecture of Domestic Wonder," in *Tom Kundig Houses 2*
    (New York: Princeton Architectural Press, 2011, pp. 217–24),
    p. 220.

2   Maggie and Scottie Greene, interview with author. San
    Juan Island, Washington. July 2013.

3   Friedman, p. 22.

4

Ravine Guest House

Shim-Sutcliffe

Ravine Guest House
Shim-Sutcliffe

Don Mills, Canada   43.7°N, 79.3°W   2004

500 SF

FLOOR PLAN
1 entry
2 kitchen
3 bathroom
4 living room
5 bedroom
6 fireplace
7 mechanical
8 reflecting pool

Figure 4.2 Ravine Guest House view from Main House

Sited on a three-acre heavily wooded parcel abutting a ravine about ten miles north of Toronto, this project provides a serene contemplative space adjacent to the main house. This wood and glass pavilion is a "glowing lantern" in the ravine forest, surrounded by a lush landscape of mature red pines and black locust trees.

The journey to the Ravine Guest House is by foot down a winding gravel path. A slatted wooden bridge forms the threshold to the pavilion, leading across the L-shaped reflecting pool to the generous wood-planked terrace. The pool is planted with water lilies and bullrushes creating a rich water landscape surrounded by a verdant and distinctive Toronto ravine landscape.

Intended as a quiet retreat, the program for the project has both indoor and outdoor elements. The indoor program includes a bedroom, a sitting room, a bathroom, and a kitchen that can serve as a catering area for larger functions. The

outdoor program includes a large wooden deck, a reflecting pool, a covered dining area, and a long concrete countertop for storage of firewood and garden equipment.

A deliberate ambiguity is created between what is interior and what is exterior, as elements are interwoven to create a series of interlocking spaces. A large central indoor-outdoor fireplace reinforces this ambiguity; it has a sliding fire-glass window between the two fireboxes, permitting a separation between inside and out while allowing views through one to the other.

Facing west, large wood and glass doors unfold, allowing the building's main living and sleeping space to open fully to the outdoors. A view toward the reflecting pool and terraces is framed by the remaining south wall and fireplace. Ipe wood flooring, used for the interior, extends seamlessly beyond the doors to form the deck, further extending the modest interior into the landscape and again blurring the distinction between inside and out.

Figure 4.3 Ravine Guest House interior space connects directly to exterior

above allow the ceiling plane to appear to float. The simple rectangular prism of roof and glass hovers above the hearth and the terrace, creating shade and shelter for an outdoor dining area.

Shim and Sutcliffe, established in Toronto, Ontario in 1994, continues to seek sophisticated solutions to each design problem they face. Each project embodies their commitment to an architecture that is powerfully connected to site, to a continual interpretation of program, and to constant innovation in detail resolution. The role of their numerous collaborators and the community that supports them is essential to creating not only architecture but design that contributes in a meaningful way to people's lives. The firm's principals have a shared interest and passion for the integration and interrelated scales of architecture, landscape, and furniture. Their work is redefining design practice by intertwining light, water, and landscape in exploratory and innovative ways. Their projects, both small and large, question and simultaneously engage the relationship between building and landscape, man and nature. Shim and Sutcliffe also designed the Craven Road Studio (pp. 116–21).

Structural steel and Douglas fir roof framing is fully exposed and expressed. A hanging structural frame enables the Profilit cast glass clerestory to be completely continuous overhead. The openness of the pavilion's walls, the minimalism of the structure's framing, and the glowing quality of the milky glass

OPPOSITE TOP
Figure 4.4 Ravine Guest House fireplace adjacent to sliding doors

OPPOSITE BELOW
Figure 4.5 Ravine Guest House channel glass clerestory and wood framed roof supported by steel beams

5

Writer's Studio
Cooper Joseph Studio

Writer's Studio
Cooper Joseph Studio

Ghent, NY   42.3°N, 73.6°W   2007
525 SF

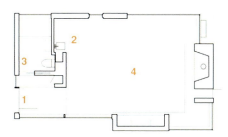

FLOOR PLAN
1 entry
2 pantry
3 bathroom
4 studio

Figure 5.2 Writer's Studio south elevation

This small studio, located in a deciduous forest in upstate New York, provides a special place for one person to read, write, listen to music, and gaze out towards several framed views. Each orientation has a different set of openings to allow for variable light and specific views. To the west, windows open onto a clearing while views to the north face the densely wooded site. The studio is a "bespoke suit" for its owner.

The studio's structure, a simple box eroded with large corner windows, is built entirely with wood framing. Entry is from the south through a wide glass pivot door that leads to a tall entry hall with a wall of ribbon windows on one side and a wood-clad wall on the other. Highly polished walnut floors are used throughout the space, providing what appears as a seamless continuous plane that reflects the light. Narrow horizontal slats of walnut clad the interior walls, giving a refined unit of measure to the space. Walnut, a prevalent wood species in the eastern United States, provides a straight regular grain and good dimensional stability, and it is a favorite of the architects due to its workability and warm tones. Custom sliding doors and furniture are made of solid walnut, as is,

remarkably, the bathroom sink. An array of grooves cut into the wood sink allows for drainage. Larger grooves at the center of the sink, right below the waterspout, provide more void space to accept and move the water to the drain. Grooves at the edge of the sink are smaller and spaced closer to form a more continuous countertop surface. The other predominant interior material—aside from large panels of glass—is black slate, used in the form of pebbles, split face stone, and horizontal tile. In the bathroom, a wall of glass in the shower provides views to pond and meadow beyond.

Two elements help anchor the minimally detailed open space. One is a highly sculptural, custom-designed walnut desk that sits atop the reflective walnut floors. The other is a large fireplace with a surround of slate pebbles that serves as a visual and structural anchor for the studio. Large glass panels located in the cantilevered corners on either side of the fireplace blur the distinction between interior and exterior. The exterior is clad with cedar siding using both flat, wide boards and thinner slats. An ebony black stain clarifies the project metaphorically as "a shadow in the woods."

Figure 5.3 Writer's Studio east elevation

Cooper Joseph Studio is located in New York City where they design residential, public, and exhibition projects. The architects of Cooper Joseph Studio have a distinctive way of designing; they always start with the boldest, most profound strategy and work to maintain a reductive vocabulary as the project develops from sketch to finished building. They have no standard boilerplate solution to architectural problems, a distinct advantage of their small-scale practice.

While there are natural materials that they love to use, they rarely go back to those materials in the same way from project to project. The firm is most mindful that a small house should feel intimate but not restricted. Tall volumes help create a feeling of openness and allow rooms to share space with the landscape beyond. Cooper Joseph Studio also designed the Small House in an Olive Grove (pp. 94–9).

OPPOSITE TOP
Figure 5.4 Writer's Studio fireplace weights the end of highly polished walnut floor

OPPOSITE BELOW
Figure 5.5 Writer's Studio entry into tall narrow volume

6

Hill Country Jacal

Lake/Flato

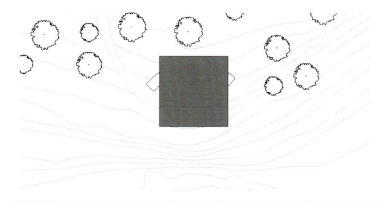

Hill Country Jacal

Lake/Flato

Pipe Creek, Texas   29.7°N, 98.9°W   1997

925 SF

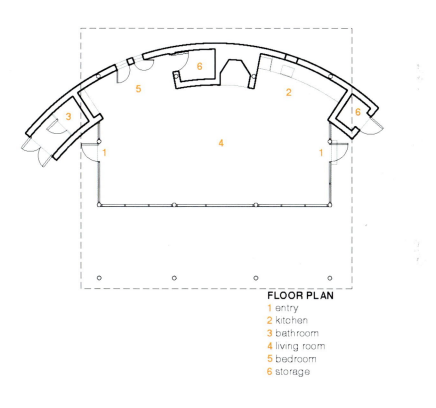

FLOOR PLAN
1 entry
2 kitchen
3 bathroom
4 living room
5 bedroom
6 storage

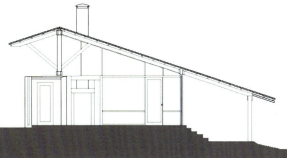

Figure 6.2 Hill Country Jacal design sketch

Figure 6.3 Hill Country Jacal roof follows the slope of the land

This weekend house sits very lightly on the land and, if left unattended, could become a ruin by design. The house is self-sustaining with regard to water and electricity; photovoltaics provide electricity and the roof directs the capture of rainwater. This simple shelter "deals with conditions that have always existed."[1] The form reflects an understanding of vernacular structures and recollects the architect's fond childhood memories of working with the climate. He recalls, as a child, using a water hose to cool down the hot metal roof of a simple one-room weekend cabin during the hot Texas summers.

This site, located forty miles northwest of San Antonio, slopes gently toward a running creek. The location is close enough to home to be able to drive to safety if the weather gets too wild. The building, conceived of as a simple non-air-conditioned shelter that allows the occupants to be "in the weather" most of the year, utilizes strategies for working with the weather and enhancing the prevailing south breeze. The clients—the Caseys, friends and neighbors of architect Ted Flato—were very much part of the design team and made thoughtful

compromises to keep the scope of the project focused. This project was not simply about being small but about doing only what was needed to create a place for fun activities for the family. The overall attitude and simplified program of this project were decided on very quickly. Flato describes "leading the witness" over lunch to focus on a straightforward solution that embraced the idea of camping.

The structure reinterprets the overall form of a jacal, a traditional "lean-to" found in the Southwest, but using stone in lieu of the more typical mud infill. This thick curving stone wall protects the inhabitants from cold northern winds and defines the zone for the bath, kitchen, and solar cell batteries. As Flato likes to say, there is even space to "store the kids"—in bunk beds tucked in a nook. A highly insulated shed roof shields the interior space from the harsh Texas sun and extends to create a covered porch on the south side of the building. Large flaps, located above the sheltering wall, face north and can be opened or closed to regulate both airflow and light quantity inside.

Figure 6.4 Hill Country Jacal entrance to outdoor shower

Figure 6.5 Hill Country Jacal view from the north

The materials used are very familiar to the architecture team and were found within minutes of the site. The solid stone wall is made from locally quarried limestone. Columns are site-harvested cedar. Simple insect screening, held in place with standard dimensional lumber that sits in front of the wobbly columns, makes up most of the exterior surfaces. The screen wall, disengaged from the rather crude columns, is attached to a dimensional lumber frame to allow the screen to float in front of the columns, providing a continuous yet very porous wrapping.

Thinking about how to actually build the house came first; the overall process needed to be thoughtful and efficient. The materials the design team selected are ones that they knew well and that could be found locally and immediately—anything precious or having a long lead time would not work. They also knew that not just any contractor could be used for such a small house. William Orr, a friend with whom they had worked on several past projects, had the skill set that equaled the detailing requirements of this project. The owners began the initial research for the catchment and photovoltaic systems, giving them both responsibility and full participation in the project. This way of creating true ownership of the

project for the clients also simplified the balancing of budget issues for the newer technologies and assured that they would know how the systems work.

The quality of light inside the space is a direct result of thinking about wind, weather, and views in equal measure. Luckily, the land slopes to the southwest, along with the best views of the running creek. Generous overhangs on all sides help "keep the sun at bay"[2] and allow the interior space to be bathed in light. The north-facing flaps also allow for modest adjustments to interior light levels.

The goal of being electrically self-sustaining allowed energy and science to drive some decisions. Everything was considered in order to minimize energy use, battery expense, and storage requirements. The decision to use propane-powered kitchen appliances reduced electrical consumption and further simplified the design process due to the limited choices of propane appliances.

This weekend house, although designed for a family, also supports gatherings of larger groups for entertaining. The main room is quite large yet scaled to allow dining at one end,

Figure 6.6 Hill Country Jacal fireplace and kitchen along north wall

sleeping at the other, and hanging out in between. Everything inside has multiple purposes: the kitchen table doubles as an island, and the bed is on wheels so it can be easily moved to change the function of the room when desired. The big roof steps down the hill and covers this straightforward flexible space that is deeply connected to the outdoors.

Lake/Flato was established in San Antonio, Texas in 1984. Founding partners Ted Flato and David Lake continue the work of the internationally acclaimed firm, designing buildings at a variety of scales, types, and locations. Flato finds that

having a small budget or size can often be an asset in a residential project. Typically, a million-dollar budget does not necessitate a homeowner to make the drastic compromises or suffer the inconveniences required to build something simple.

Notes

1 Ted Flato, interview with author. San Antonio, Texas. December 2013.
2 Flato.

Kemper Cabin
Suyama Peterson Deguchi

Skagit County, Washington   48.5°N, 121.8°W   1992

1000 SF

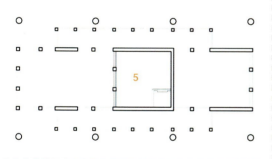

UPPER LEVEL

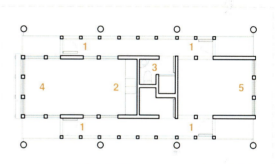

GROUND LEVEL

FLOOR PLANS
1 entry
2 kitchen
3 bathroom
4 living room
5 bedroom

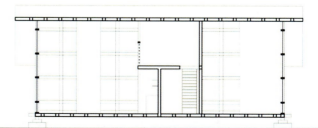

Figure 7.2 Kemper Cabin detail of wood joinery

For this cabin in Skagit County, Washington, architect George Suyama had a client and builder with a willingness to try something new. The Kempers had owned a forty-acre property since 1986 and often camped on the special site, buffered on the east by trees but opening up to the west and adjacent to a national research reserve. The project required a leap of faith, both in definition of comfort and in construction techniques. The house was built by Dale Brotherton, almost entirely out of hand-planed western red cedar, and without nails, screws, or metal attachments other than the steel cables that provide lateral support. This limited palette of materials denotes the Pacific Northwest style as well as Suyama's "wish to simplify, to eliminate visual noise."[1]

The means of construction influenced the degree of thermal comfort afforded the inhabitants. The house is constructed without any insulation, allowing the house to feel more elemental and connected to nature. As Suyama explained: "we expect to always be comfortable; we seek 'experiences' when

we are on vacation but require an almost numbing comfort"[2] at home.

The simple gable roof, its underside enclosing the 20-foot-tall main room, focuses the view and provides shelter in the form of a "permanent tent." Instead of solid walls, a wood frame is used to enclose space. The structure is primitive to the point that it feels elemental and helps to answer the question: how little can you do and still feel sheltered? In addition to having no insulation, the house also has no source of heat. The owners move up to the loft to be closer to the warmest air. As noted by Lisa Heschong, "[thermal] uniformity is extremely unnatural and therefore requires a great deal of effort, and energy, to maintain."[3] Suyama's interest in ecological concerns is also supported by his agreement that "the more senses that are involved in a particular experience, the fuller and rounder, the experience becomes."[4] This house does not control light; it interferes only minimally with the natural illumination. In addition to doing very little to control the movement of heat, the house also does little to control sound. The thin structure of the screened galleries allows movement from one space to the next and acts as an amplifier of birds' songs outside. Moveable panels provide varying degrees of enclosure as one circulates through these galleries. The minimal intervention acts to increase the physical experience. There is little separation between inhabitants and environment while the architecture amplifies the experience.

The architecture firm Suyama Peterson Deguchi was founded in 1971 and is based in Seattle. Suyama's larger projects and modernist work often incorporates a modular system of organization, yet his working method changes when engaged in smaller projects. Suyama has found that what might work in a larger house often must be thrown out for smaller projects. A house cannot merely be scaled down from 3,000 square feet to 1,000 square feet. Designing smaller houses requires critical reconsideration, rethinking the whole problem, and discovering what is truthful. Since man is "genetically the same as when we first started walking upright,"[5] argues Suyama, architects must connect to that genetic base. We get close when designing a modest dwelling. Suyama's thoughts resonate with the words of Le Corbusier from 1923: "all people have the same organism, the same functions, the same needs."[6]

Suyama lived, with his wife and two cats, in a 550-square-foot cabin for four and a half years while designing and building his current house. Physically experiencing living in a small space might be necessary to conceive of or even allow it. Suyama also finds camping a useful metaphor when considering a small house. Camping is a release from our everyday world, and, using it as a metaphor, it can free us to see new ways to solve problems. Architects can focus on designing for singular issues such as getting out of the rain, listening to the rain, or sitting under a tree. Understanding scale change in a small house is also important. Suyama recalls visiting a Frank Lloyd Wright house many years ago. The vestibule had a mere 7-foot ceiling and the space then "exploded" to about 10 feet. He recalls it as a very dramatic and very appropriate scale shift.

Figure 7.3 Kemper Cabin bedroom on the east side of the cabin

Figure 7.4 Kemper Cabin looking out through living room from loft

Figure 7.5 Kemper Cabin next to forest

Notes

1 Grant Hildebrand. *Suyama: A Complex Serenity*. (Seattle: Marquand Books, 2011), p. 11.

2 George Suyama, interview with author. Seattle, Washington. August 2013.

3 Lisa Heschong. *Thermal Delight in Architecture*. (Cambridge: MIT Press, 1989), p. 20. A delightful book given to me by my master's thesis advisor, Gerald Maffei, which I have read repeatedly over the years. This book is tiny and has big ideas about thermal comfort.

4 Heschong, p. 29.

5 Suyama.

6 Le Corbusier, *Vers Une Architecture*. (Paris: Flammarion, 2012: revised edition, first published 1923).

Variant TWO
Focused Dwellings

These dwellings are often focused on a particular view or even on celestial events. While some areas of the dwelling are very protected, they also readily open to the environment. These small buildings mediate between connecting to the landscape or local context and providing a safe retreat.

Marfa 10×10

Candid Rogers Studio

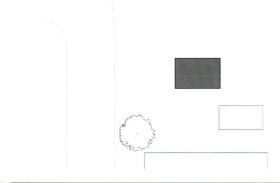

Marfa 10x10
Candid Rogers Studio

Marfa, Texas   30.32°N, 104.0°W   2007

320 SF

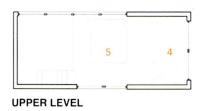

UPPER LEVEL

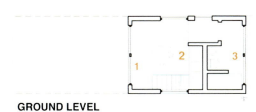

GROUND LEVEL

FLOOR PLANS
1 entry
2 kitchen
3 bathroom
4 living room
5 bedroom

Figure 8.2 Marfa 10×10 in snow

Marfa, located in the high desert of West Texas, with a population of less than two thousand, is home to multiple generations of ranchers as well as many newcomers who are bringing art and design interests to this dusty community. At the southeastern edge of town, less than a fifteen-minute walk from the central courthouse, a new resident is staking a claim in this often intense climate. The top priority for this client was minimizing the construction trades by utilizing simplified assemblies while providing a shaded spot in this hot, dry climate.

The roughness of the steel exterior communicates the solidity and safety of the enclosure. The materials used in this project are as rugged and unrelenting as the West Texas landscape. Cor-ten steel clads the simple extended wood-framed box. The literal and visual weight of the exterior cladding material contrasts with the highly finished birch plywood used for flooring and cabinetry on the protected interior. A lightweight aluminum ship ladder stair continues the contrast between the visual and literal lightness inside and the heft of the exterior.

This compact small house simultaneously extends and connects to the jagged landscape beyond. The building apertures are oriented to maximize natural light with the largest openings facing the mountain ranges to the north. Openings to the east and west are minimized in order to reduce the admittance of the harsh horizontal sun. The long walls have a few skinny horizontal slit windows, along with the operable south-facing doors, to allow for cross ventilation. In this remote landscape, at—what feels like—the very edge of civilization, the steel-clad volume defines a domesticated space.

Custom-made doors, with hinges at the top, flip up to provide the desired degree of connectivity or enclosure.

Figure 8.3 Marfa 10×10 cantilevered box faces the mountains

The north-facing second level cantilevers and stretches to the view toward the mountains. A thin delicate steel shade structure extends to the south, providing an easy gathering spot. This shaded trellis also relates to the interior scale. The connection to outside and the framing of particular views was as important as providing maximum shading.

Originally planned as a weekend getaway, this is now a nearly full-time residence for the clients. Once they experienced the space they realized that everything was accounted for; they could live this way for longer periods of time and they now get by better with less. Perhaps less can be more!

Candid Rogers Studio was formed in 2004 in San Antonio, Texas, and concentrates on residential and small commercial work. When working on a small project, Rogers often focuses first on designing the areas of primary use, such as sleeping

and living spaces. His intuition and past experience help him understand what is the least amount of room or the minimum dimension that you can get by with and still have it work for practical use. Thinking about these issues of scale from the very beginning and planning as efficiently as possible is essential for a small house. Once Rogers has the right spatial sequence and connection to the landscape, a small project also demands that he look at the details and materials. Particular assemblies will determine the minimum thickness of the exterior envelope, which, in a small project, really does matter. Fixed costs and overhead further can contribute to making the project cost per square foot much greater for a small house since some costs are not determined by scale. Mobilization, starting of construction, and travel to the site are not directly related to the scope of the project. Though most of his clients want more space, rather than less, budget constraints often help to reprioritize goals.

Figure 8.4 Marfa 10×10 kitchen with loft above

Figure 8.5 Marfa 10×10 looking in from under the trellis

9

Keenan Tower House

Marlon Blackwell Architect

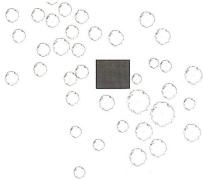

Keenan Tower House

Marlon Blackwell Architect

Fayetteville, Arkansas   36.1°N, 94.2°W   2000

560 SF

LEVEL 1

LEVEL 2

LEVEL 3

LEVEL 4

LEVEL 5

LEVEL 6

FLOOR PLANS
1 entry
2 mechanical
3 bathroom
4 living room
5 sky court

Figure 9.2 Keenan Tower House looking down the interior of the stairs

The clients, a young couple, requested a tree house to afford views of the foothills of the Ozark Mountains. However, a study of the site revealed that none of the site trees was large enough to support a living space. After Marlon Blackwell visited Yemen, where he saw many stacked houses, he developed this tower solution. Its 82 foot height profile is a modern reconsideration of nearby industrial towers and grain silos. It is both alien and familiar in this rural setting in northwest Arkansas.

Both the intimacy of the interior space and the immensity of the place were considered as the circulation sequence was developed. A series of stair runs wrap around a hollow core that hugs the interior face of the tower's exterior skin. The first habitable space on the ascension route contains a bathroom and a space for a sink and small refrigerator. Two punctured windows frame specific views to the vast countryside. The middle, enclosed floor is wrapped on all four sides by glass,

allowing panoramic views. A hatch in the ceiling on this level leads to the top level "sky court." This is essentially an exterior space shielded on two sides by solid walls and open to the east, west, and sky above. Views here are no longer panoramic and are more heavily orchestrated by the architect to clarify celestial relationships.

Blackwell is interested in how materials are distributed within a project. Typically, each project focuses on a limited number of ordinary materials—or materials used in unusual ways. The exact material palette is determined by the site location and the specific requirements of the project. Here, the steel structure is wrapped in horizontal standing seam metal cladding with locally milled white oak fins around the staircase. Both the metal skin and the wood cladding visually connect to agricultural buildings nearby yet are transformed by either scale or juxtaposition to allow the materials to be seen as something new. Interior materials

Figure 9.3 Keenan Tower House middle level looking at treetops

include white oak flooring, limited use of maple, and planar gypsum board walls. The white oak reappears in the sky court, framing the extra-large views at a very human and familiar scale. Each material connects to the rural setting while reinterpreting scale.

Rather than focusing on bringing in as much light as possible, Blackwell used various strategies to avoid allowing too much light in the space. He specifically wanted to achieve a balanced relationship between light and shadow. On the middle level, light is brought in across the ceiling plane from all four sides to allow it to be graduated and always changing. White walls help reflect and diffuse light throughout the space. The openings in the building each face the cardinal directions, which also aids in orienting inhabitants to the land, season, day, and year.

The project was designed to be a perch from which weather and the cosmos could be observed. The view from upper levels extends for miles in the surrounding rural landscape. The experience of the weather is intensified from the interior, and approaching storms can be viewed in the distance. On the equinox, when sitting in the sky court, the full moon can be seen rising in the eastern sky while the sun is setting in the western sky—with both in the same position on the horizon. The structure allows both distant and opposing phenomena to be brought into one space.

Marlon Blackwell Architect is located in Fayetteville, Arkansas, where Blackwell teaches and runs his diverse practice that is engaged with modern vernacular investigations at multiple scales. Blackwell's work focuses on the relationship of building to land, explores how the structure meets the land, and examines the dialogue between the nature-made and the man-made. This building, while smaller in terms of the size of its enclosure than most of Blackwell's work, shows how even a diminutive footprint can provide a majestic perch.

Figure 9.4 Keenan Tower House focused views from the top level Sky Court

Figure 9.5 Keenan Tower House the tower in the landscape

10

Sky Ranch

The Miller Hull Partnership

Sky Ranch

The Miller Hull Partnership

Seattle, Washington   47.6°N, 122.3°W   2007

800 SF

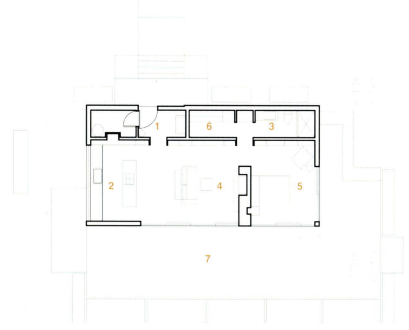

FLOOR PLAN
1 entry
2 kitchen
3 bathroom
4 living room
5 bedroom
6 storage
7 deck

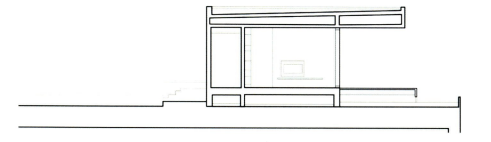

Figure 10.2 Sky Ranch house is perched on warehouse roof

This small 800-square-foot residence sits directly on top of an immense 62,000-square-foot warehouse roof "site" looking out on the unobstructed view of the working marina in Seattle's Ballard area. The juxtaposition of small-scale domesticity in an industrialized urban setting provides an example of how one might live fully in such a unique neighborhood. The zoning regulations allow for a "caretaker's unit" in an otherwise industrial zone. For Scott Wolf, the partner in charge of this project, this project offers a way to increase urban density through the inhabitation of these forgotten "landscapes."

The building is wrapped in vertical corrugated metal cladding, helping it to fit in with its warehouse neighbors. The metal skin also reflects light, making the perched dwelling appear even lighter and more ephemeral. Interior finishes of warm wood connect the space to the lumber industry of the Pacific Northwest, as well as providing a domestic feel for the interior

in such an industrialized setting. The wood flooring was selected as much for its light weight as for its visual and tactile warmth. Originally, the client had requested concrete floors; but because this project sits on top of another building, the physical weight of the materials was a real consideration. The original structure was reinforced to accommodate the new building.

Adequate access to light is at a premium in Seattle where there might be just seventy clear and sunny days a year. The large openings wrap around the east-, south-, and west-facing walls and are lifted all the way to the ceiling in order to allow the diffuse light from the often-cloudy sky to penetrate deep into the space.

The clarity of the plan—service spaces including the bathroom and 20 feet of storage are organized along the north wall—gives a sparseness and generosity to the

Figure 10.3 Sky Ranch covered wood deck looks towards the marina

living space. The north-facing solid wall offers protection from northern winds and the eyes of the city, allowing the large openings to the deck and marina beyond to be extended by the large overhang that defines an exterior space on top of the vast roof. Because the roof "site" actually amplifies the wind and the sun, deep porch overhangs, window shades, and solid north wall help protect the occupants.

The laundry, dressing, and bath are arranged along one long wall. A fireplace and built-in storage separate the private sleeping area from the public living, dining, and kitchen. In this minimal dwelling, the generous storage space and two large wood decks support big living within a small space.

The client of Sky Ranch also owns the Stimson Marina, on whose roof the small dwelling is now perched. The client had

originally desired the house to be prefabricated. However, the cost of a crane to lift the unit helped determine that the project would be built on-site yet still appear to be relocatable. "Little houses and smaller spaces have real charm and appeal," Wolf said. "They force you to be more conscious about what you have in your life and how you live in your residence."[1] Wolf speaks from personal experiences; he once lived in a 500-square-foot house.

The Miller Hull Partnership, established in Seattle in 1977, primarily focuses on public, institutional, or commercial

OPPOSITE TOP
Figure 10.4 Sky Ranch kitchen with full wall of storage

OPPOSITE BELOW
Figure 10.5 Sky Ranch living room with covered deck on the right

projects, yet the firm has designed several small houses. When designing small houses, they often find ways to shave off the size of spaces with different furniture placements. In bedrooms, the fixed size of the bed is a challenge; yet if it is pushed up against a window, it becomes an intimate part of the window and the size of the bedroom can be decreased.[2] Building in furniture and storage is another favorite tactic. They might lay out a space for a client and actually tape off space on the floor in order to help them focus on efficiency. Founding partner Robert Hull[3] spent many weekends in a 1930s cabin without running water, electricity, or cell service. He found it delightful and hopefully instructive as the firm—which recently completed the Bullitt Center in Seattle, considered by many to be the world's greenest office building—prepares to design more net zero projects, some at the residential scale.

Notes

1   Mikoto Ohtake, "Sky Small," *Dwell* magazine, May 2010.
2   Robert Hull, interview with author. Seattle, Washington. July 2012.
3   Sadly, Robert Hull recently passed away. Hull, along with his long-standing business partner David Miller, led The Miller Hull Partnership to national prominence as a leader in the practice of Pacific Northwest regional design. He was very gracious and generous with his time with me.

Scholar's Library

GLUCK +

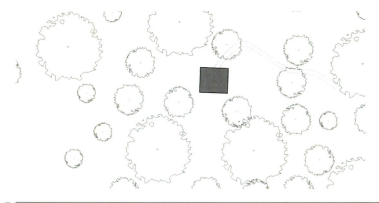

Scholar's Library
GLUCK+

Upstate New York   2003

800 SF

UPPER LEVEL

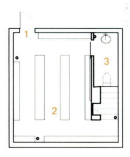

GROUND LEVEL

FLOOR PLANS
1 entry
2 book stacks
3 bathroom
4 study

Figure 11.2 Scholar's Library second floor writing studio with windows open in spring

Located two hours north of Manhattan, on a heavily wooded site near a reservoir, this simple form sits directly on the ground. It appears as an unexpected folly in the forest. The client, a scholar of Japanese history (and wife of the architect) originally requested a new chair for her desk. The new chair project quickly became a new desk project. Soon, the really hard question "what are you going to do with all of these books?"[1] was asked, and the program requirements gradually became a new library and writing studio.

Peter Gluck designed and built this project on family property in upstate New York. A house for his son—the Tower House, an elegant suspended box supported by a glass stair tower—was also recently built on the same property. For this building, Gluck looked to clues from the site and the program in order to achieve a harmony between the two. In this clear, lucid project, the overall form signifies the use of the building. As Gluck describes, "the study sits on the books below, much like scholarship rests on the body of work that precedes it."[2] The ground floor, thermally controlled, provides a protected environment for the storage of the scholar's book collection. Very little natural light is allowed to enter the space in order to protect the books from possible UV damage. The upper level, a completely open, light-filled writing studio, is lifted up and removed from the floor of the forest. It provides a place of speculation and study.

The Platonic cube building sits in the underbrush of the densely treed site and thus receives no direct light. During summer months, its sliding panels—actually standard sliding glass doors used as windows—can be opened up on all four sides, turning it into a screened loft space with summer breezes filtering through and immersing the writer in the natural world of the forest. A thin roof extends over the volume and appears to almost float. The white ceiling reflects light, creating a diffusely lit, contemplative environment for the writer.

Figure 11.3 Scholar's Library second floor writing studio in winter

Major materials include steel, glass, maple flooring, and dark cementitious panels that clad the lower level, allowing it to mimic the surrounding shadowy forest. The project is protected by the canopy of the trees and receives only filtered light. The bottom level reflects the darkness of the trees' understory and is meant to appear completely enclosed and lightless. This lower level is secret and secure, disengaged from the ground plane. The Minerit cement panels are detailed to make the entry door location not readily clear. In contrast, the upper level connects to the trees and becomes a screened room when all the glass panels are slid away from the corners.

Steel columns support the roof and the ceiling that hovers at the open corners.

Peter Gluck runs an architect-led design-build practice based in New York City. The firm, GLUCK +, builds most of its own projects. Constructability runs in their blood. From day one of a new project, they start to think about how to build what they design. The same team works on the entire building project, from design to construction, helping elevate quality and reduce cost for the client, while linking creativity and responsibility.

Figure 11.4 Scholar's Library lower level book collection storage

Figure 11.5 Scholar's Library hidden entry door is located to the left

Notes

1   Peter Gluck, phone interview with author. January 2014.
2   Gluck.

12

Roland Cabin

David Salmela

Roland Cabin
David Salmela

La Pointe, Wisconsin   46.8°N, 90.8°W   2009

810 SF

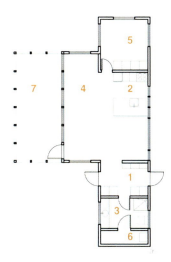

FLOOR PLAN
1 entry
2 kitchen
3 bathroom
4 living room
5 bedroom
6 storage
7 screen porch

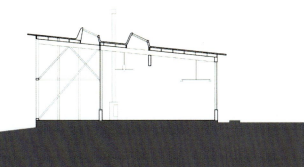

Figure 12.2 Roland Cabin entry from the east

The cabin, situated on Madeline Island, acts as a retreat for the clients, a family of four who live full-time in Minneapolis. Most weekends—after four hours of driving and a short ferry ride—they land in a place with great vegetation, trees, and very little disruption of land.

This cabin was rebuilt on the same footprint as the previous structure, which was falling down and in disrepair. Because the project was considered a remodel, the new building could be built at the original location, closer to the lake than new buildings are permitted to build. This existing footprint, however, also provided an additional set of constraints.

The exterior is clad in Skatelite by Richlite, a paper resin product that is inert and cannot be coated. Skatelite is often used for skateboard ramps and is very durable, even in the harsh Wisconsin winters. The asphalt color helps the cabin blend into the shadows of the woods, and the exterior is virtually maintenance-free. All exterior trim is cedar that is left to age, with only the sauna door requiring paint. Aluminum-clad windows, flashing and a low-profile EPDM roof help keep the snow and weather out. Interior walls are clad with local basswood installed in random widths. Not only does this cladding create a fairly lively pattern on the interior, but the wood species and random sizes are also just a quarter the price of recycled Douglas fir.

David Salmela believes that rooms, especially living spaces, need as much light as possible, coming from as many directions as possible. He hypothesizes that this is a problem with most hotel rooms: no matter how luxurious the appointments are, hotel rooms are never quite comfortable due to the fact that light is coming from only one direction. In the Roland Cabin, several skylights, including two in the screened porch, help bring in additional light. The roof of the living space is high and sloped up, which allows large windows to also provide light from above. Specific Archimide fixtures, with adjustable light levels, bring in a warm light in the evening.

The house, basically a rectangular bar with a widening in the living area, has a screened-in porch on the south side, facing Lake Superior. By connecting the screened porch directly to the cabin, with no door directly to the outside that might allow the bugs in, means that none of the windows along that edge need screens. The delicate frame-like quality of the porch appears to be buttressed by a strong, dark, bar building that provides a contrasting backdrop. A bathroom and utility core at one end, closest to the entry, allows the rest of the simple box volume to be used for flexible activities. How one enters a space is as important to Salmela as it was to Alvar Aalto. Aalto described the act of entering buildings in a harsh (Nordic) climate as "require[ing] a sharp differentiation between the warm interior and the surroundings."[1] The straightforwardness

Figure 12.3 Roland Cabin porch with views of Lake Superior

of the design is reflective of Salmela's Scandinavian roots and years of Midwestern winters.

Salmela Architect is based in Duluth, Minnesota, and primarily designs residential projects. Salmela starts all projects, regardless of scale, with questions about the site. He documents the location of the sun, views, breezes, and movement on the site. How one enters the site—the first impression—is important, but does not trump the relationship of the building to light and wind. As he starts sketching and getting to know the program, the concept becomes clear. He likes to move to hard-lined dimensional drawings very early, moving from plan to section to elevation. He also likes to meet with clients as soon as possible to make sure

everything is going in the right direction. Once the design problem is solved, he makes a model to verify and check the design. Salmela would again agree with his predecessor who advised architects: "Don't do anything stilted, don't do anything unnecessary. Everything that is superfluous becomes ugly with time."[2] Salmela's buildings are designed with simplicity, appropriateness, and beautiful slow-paced weathering in mind.

Notes

1   Goran Schildt, *Alvar Aalto: The Early Years* (New York: Rizzoli, 1984), p. 215.
2   Goran Schildt, p. 205.

OPPOSITE TOP
Figure 12.4 Roland Cabin looking towards entry and mud room

OPPOSITE BELOW
Figure 12.5 Roland Cabin living room looking towards kitchen with bedroom beyond

13

Small House in an Olive Grove

Cooper Joseph Studio

Small House in an Olive Grove
Cooper Joseph Studio

Geyserville, California 38.7°N, 122.9°W 2010

850 SF

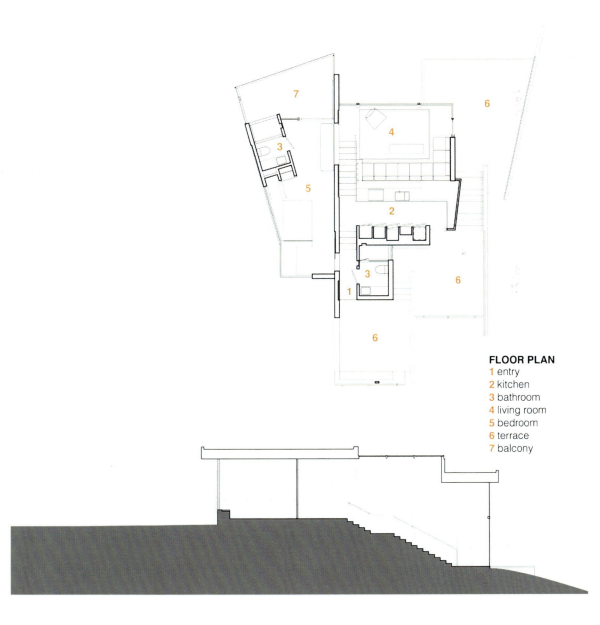

FLOOR PLAN
1 entry
2 kitchen
3 bathroom
4 living room
5 bedroom
6 terrace
7 balcony

Figure 13.2 Small House in an Olive Grove north elevation at night

Two scientists requested a small, sustainable dwelling that takes advantage of the views from their 25-acre property in northern California's Sonoma Valley. Sustainability criteria led to the minimal footprint, energy-efficient systems, and improved site infrastructure, which includes a solar array that now provides power to the entire property, buildings, and equipment.

The small house has just two distinct interior spaces yet has three cascading exterior terraces, each descending with the sloping site and increasing the perceived size of the interior space. The modest entrance is located in the solid southern facade under a large covered porch. Inside, the house is incredibly open with abundant light and views. The bedroom and living room both face north and are open to the landscape. The majority of the windows have north-facing glass, bringing in diffused light, while south-facing glass is protected by overhangs or horizontal redwood louvers. On-axis circulation has focused views to the valley and leads between articulated living areas in the house. On one side of the distinctive central concrete wall is the bedroom, on the same level as the entry. It features a narrow

daybed set underneath a horizontal interior window that looks down into the living room below. A balcony at the northern edge of the bedroom provides a shaded place for contemplation. On the other side of the central wall, the kitchen—down a few steps from the entry level—has a small eating counter and a direct connection to a large exterior dining terrace designed for entertaining. The kitchen looks through the living room's tall volume to the olive grove beyond. Down another half flight of stairs, on the lowest level of the house, is the living room, which is both grand and intimate.

Concrete walls and rigid steel framing support a micro-laminated wood roof structure. Concrete retaining walls are embedded into the hill and protect exterior areas of the house. These splayed walls define the overall composition and extend the views out to the landscape. The window system includes custom profiles, engineered for seismic loading, with mullions recessed into the floor and ceiling to allow for a direct connection of the interior and exterior. The resulting assembly makes for a simplified composition of solid and void with all details abstracted.

Figure 13.3 Small House in an Olive Grove living room looking east

The architects used natural materials that weather well under the strong California sun. The load-bearing concrete walls are left exposed with the graining of the plywood formwork imprinted on the surface. Zinc, in horizontal panels, is used to clad much of the exterior walls. The projected 100-year life span of zinc matches the strength of concrete. French limestone, used for centuries due to its durability and versatility, also complements the adjacent concrete. On the interior, it is used in elongated pieces set in a horizontal running bond pattern for the floors throughout the house. Grey stained oak, with inserts of clear resin to catch passing sunlight, is used for cabinetry fronts and wall paneling in the kitchen and living room.

In this meticulously detailed house, the composition of the exterior elements in the landscape is as important as the interior spaces. The clients are beekeepers, so all plantings are bee-friendly. Fields of lavender and rosemary create large monocultures on the site. The architects created strong spatial relationships between landscape and interior spaces, carrying the hillside contours between them.

Cooper Joseph Studio feels that the beginning phases of a small project might be completed more quickly than on a larger one, yet the basic architectural questions are the same, no matter the scale. A small house should not feel tight, so it is important to make at least one room embrace gracious proportion. In this efficient, compact home, it is the living room, with its custom built-in furnishings, playful recesses, and expansive views that provide the desired generosity of space. Cooper Joseph Studio also designed the Writer's Studio (pp. 32–7).

OPPOSITE TOP
Figure 13.4 Small House in an Olive Grove living room looking north
OPPOSITE BELOW
Figure 13.5 Small House in an Olive Grove bedroom with daybed and balcony

14

Stacked Cabin

Johnsen Schmaling Architects

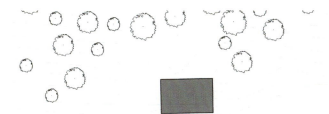

Stacked Cabin
Johnsen Schmaling Architects

Muscoda, Wisconsin   43.2°N, 90.5°W   2012

880 SF

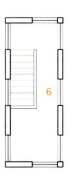

THIRD LEVEL

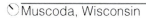

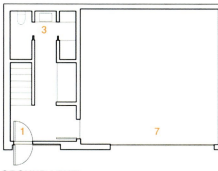

GROUND LEVEL

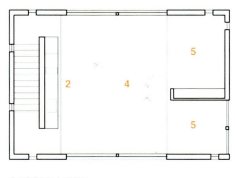

SECOND LEVEL

FLOOR PLANS
1 entry
2 kitchen
3 bathroom
4 living room
5 bedroom
6 study
7 garage

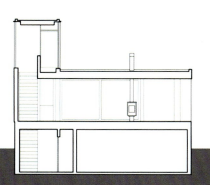

Figure 14.2 Stacked Cabin sits on a sloped site

The clients—a young family—often camped on this sloping, rural site in southwestern Wisconsin, a little more than an hour west of Madison, before they asked Johnsen Schmaling Architects to provide a "place to cook and a place to sleep."[1] Vertically stacking the cabin's program provides privacy and separation between the storage and bathroom on the first floor and the space for the family on the second floor. The third floor is an observatory that doubles as a study or a guest bedroom in the green canopy of the trees, removed from family life and any snoring below. On the second floor—which is the main living floor—the bedroom size determined the overall layout, with curtains separating the space, allowing for reconfiguring for daytime uses. In this way, nothing else is needed; no space is required for circulation or for the thickness of walls. Every inch is usable space. The washroom on the first floor is a deliberately stripped-down, austere place in which no one will linger, which allows one bathroom to be shared easily by many.

The exterior is clad with dark cementitious plaster with integral color and large glass panels. The panels are the largest size that can be fabricated and are exactly the size of the room. This maximum dimension of the window units determined the size and proportions of the room. On the interior, orange-yellow fabric curtains can be pulled in front of the glass and all around the space. The architects wanted a glowing warm color to illuminate the exterior at night—perhaps for the

wildlife to enjoy. They looked at more than 100 different fabric samples before finding the right weave and color that was also flame resistant—a requirement due to the proximity to the wood-burning stove. Front doors and garage doors, set in the exposed concrete first floor base, are clad in cedar.

The big walls of glass—lift and slide doors that were made in Wisconsin—bring in light all day. The units are custom-milled by Heartland ArchiSpecs and utilize tight-fitting German hardware and one-inch-thick argon-filled insulated units with low-e coating and an integral screen. The screen allows the entire house to become a screened porch and to transform from an interior space to exterior space. The architects were purposeful about using fewer artificial light fixtures, so the overall space is darker at night; task lights are provided for reading.

Johnsen Schmaling Architects is based in Milwaukee, Wisconsin and focuses on high-end residential and commercial design. As a young firm, Johnsen Schmaling finds they need to be careful with the smaller projects they take on in order to balance workload and income streams. There is more work involved per square foot in a smaller project than on a larger one, yet the firm enjoys working at that scale when "every screw counts." These smaller projects allow them to test things at a scale that is not too risky, and

Figure 14.3 Stacked Cabin second floor living level

if something goes wrong, it is easily fixable. Having a better grasp on any risk they are accepting allows them to be more adventurous. They usually start not from a program or scale requirement, but by asking clients to provide a narrative of what they want this project to be and how they think their life will be in it. The architects then create a more normative architectural program from that narrative. They have also developed intuition and experience over the past ten years. In the beginning, they took a safer approach; but when things were built, they saw that the projects could be even smaller. Now they have the confidence to shrink the design if needed.

While they look at clever projects done by other architects, the firm also has some general rules. They are straightforward with their work and rein in the size and square feet of all their projects. Their typical building envelopes are hyper-insulated and use efficient systems, such as solar and geothermal. They consider efficiency in building performance to be as important as spatial efficiency.

Note

1   N. F. M., *Residential Architect*, March/April 2012, p. 35.

Figure 14.4 Stacked Cabin curtains separate sleeping area from living space

Figure 14.5 Stacked Cabin curtains drawn in front of kitchen

Variant THREE
Protected Dwellings

These buildings are often full-time dwellings. They offer full protection from the elements, privacy, sound mitigation, and thermal control. The inhabitant can control the light and views and, therefore, the degree of connectivity to the exterior environment.

15

Williams Cabin

Atkinson Architecture

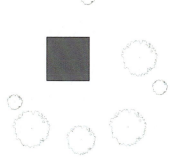

Williams Cabin
Atkinson Architecture

Durango, CO   37.3°N, 107.9°W   2008

290 SF

FLOOR PLAN
1 entry
2 kitchen
3 bathroom
4 living room/bedroom
5 covered deck

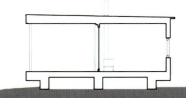

Figure 15.2 Williams Cabin porch with fire shutters at sliding doors

This cabin sits on a rugged wooded site, 7,500 feet above sea level, and facing the river valley to the west in far southwestern Colorado. The client, a music industry executive from Los Angeles, specifically requested something other than a typical log cabin and wanted the building to be both fire-resistant and sustainable. Architect Stephen Atkinson designed an abstract, white stucco square-shaped box, 24 feet by 24 feet, beneath a gently sloping metal roof. The foundation is recessed, allowing the modern white box to almost hover above the rugged site. Half of the square is devoted to the interior space of the cabin. An equal amount of space provides a covered wood deck facing the view with the small town of Durango in the distance. A stone path and a simple metal stair provide access on both sides of the deck, allowing for generous views to the landscape before entry through the sliding doors.

For this client, sustainability meant having as light an embodied footprint as possible. Using local building materials that were nontoxic and contributed to healthy indoor quality in this natural setting were prioritized. The exterior is clad with a noncombustible lime-based stucco plaster. Sustainably harvested Forest Stewardship Council-certified lumber was

used for the wood framing and plywood. The gray matte surface of the kitchen countertop is Lithistone, a locally made magnesium-based eco-ceramic concrete. The interior finish carpentry and furniture were milled from dead trees that were found on the site or cleared when making the road. Even the small stools are custom made. Plumbing fixtures, including the claw-foot tub, were found locally, reclaimed, and refinished. The concrete slab uses the maximum allowable percentage of fly ash from a nearby coal-fired power plant. Locally harvested Aspen paneling lines the interior walls and provides a lively pattern that contrasts well with the smooth uniformity of other surfaces. Eco-resin interior doors, dark red linoleum flooring, and low-VOC finishes throughout contribute to the building's healthy indoor air quality and light carbon footprint. Soy-based spray insulation, recycled denim insulation, and an efficient cast iron stove help keep the small cabin warm when needed.

Atkinson designs all of his projects with natural light in mind. The service areas of the dwelling, the kitchen and bath, are placed as far as possible to one side in order to give space for openings that admit light and views to the main living space. A string of horizontal windows runs the length of the

Figure 15.3 Williams Cabin view from above

north wall while two sets of sliding doors open onto the wood planked deck. The exterior environment is beautiful yet harsh. A cold climate, and very real danger of bears and wildfires, heightens the contrast between outside and inside. The building focuses on providing shelter and protection for the inhabitants. There are no large picture windows; the spectacular view can be enjoyed from the exterior porch. Steel fire shutters, which completely seal the house when it is unoccupied, reinforce the contrast between exterior and interior.

Stephen Atkinson is the principal at Atkinson Architecture, which is based in Palo Alto, California and focuses on residential projects. Atkinson has designed many smaller dwellings. His Zachary House of 1999, in which two rooms are bisected by a dogtrot that leads to a large deck and outdoor fireplace, is currently being reconstructed in North Carolina. He often looks to the tested layouts of boats and recreational vehicles for help in conceiving small spaces. He has also found that understanding circulation patterns is critical in making smaller spaces more useful and that proportion is often as important as size. Atkinson says he finds it far easier to design a small house than a big one, simply because there are far fewer variables to control in getting across a simple, strong idea. He readily admits that there are no scale economies in a small house. Even though the design and construction processes for a small custom dwelling are not efficient, once it is built, Atkinson says, a "small house that has a small footprint in the world is nothing but good and holy."[1]

Note

1   Stephen Atkinson, phone interview with author. December 2013.

Figure 15.4 Williams Cabin interior with custom-made furniture

Figure 15.5 Williams Cabin kitchen with reclaimed and refinished claw-foot tub beyond

Craven Road Studio

Shim-Sutcliffe

Craven Road Studio
Shim-Sutcliffe

Toronto, Ontario   43.7°N, 79.4°W   2006

560 SF

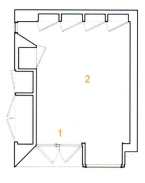

FLOOR PLAN
1 entry
2 studio

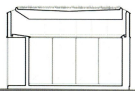

Figure 16.2 Craven Road Studio detail of coffer

This property is located east of downtown Toronto on a typical long and narrow Victorian lot. The client required a detached, freestanding studio next to his house, which could serve a variety of uses including exhibition and display, research and study, archival storage, and library shelving. Located on a tightly defined urban lot, it sits immediately adjacent to an earlier budget-driven and award-winning house that was constructed ten years ago for the same client, also designed by Shim-Sutcliffe.

One enters the site from a tranquil birch-filled court between the existing principal residence and the new studio building. A new single-car garage and 3-foot-wide walkway created for the adjacent neighbor forms the south side of the courtyard. The result is an urban ensemble of buildings flanking an outdoor open space that recontextualizes the site within the existing street edge condition defined by two-story, narrow wood siding and brick-clad gable roofed Victorian houses. The project participates in the increasing densification of the urban core while at the same time creating a tranquil and contemplative private space.

The client, a passionate collector of architectural books and graphics, stipulated that the space be lit with diffuse, indirect natural light in order to provide adequate daylighting yet avoid potential UV damage to books and archival material. An innovative system of maple-veneered, narrow light coffers surrounds the entire perimeter of the studio, varying in both rhythm and depth depending on the orientation. The series of fins forms thin coffers on the south wall that controls the abundance of light and deeper coffers on the east wall that serve as artwork storage. The incoming light washes across the face of the wood fins, providing warmth in the internal space responding to both display and working archive space. The solution is a pure collaboration between the storage function and the light requirement that simultaneously contains the three-part program of study, display, and storage.

The clear-span space is entirely column-free, and it supports a lightweight green roof planted with native grasses. The uninterrupted plane of the ceiling floats nearly 12 feet above the floor, and it slopes upward at the edge on all four sides to meet the junction of the perimeter skylight. The entrance door

Figure 16.3 Craven Road Studio interior is lit from above

is located within a setback frame with angled walls that meet the east wall at a sharp point on one side and a large projected window on the other. Adjacencies are highly specialized in what, at first glance, appears to be a simple wood-clad box.

The project's external facade responds explicitly to the principal residence. Stained marine plywood exterior cladding, installed with the grain running horizontally, relates to the wood panel walls of the existing house. The upper walls are faced with untreated cedar slats, which will weather naturally, echoing the adjacent garage and new cedar fence surrounding the property. In this modest project, every detail rigorously explores the issue of assembly.

Shim-Sutcliffe also designed the Ravine Guest House (pp. 26–31).

OPPOSITE TOP
Figure 16.4 Craven Road Studio looking out towards courtyard

OPPOSITE BELOW
Figure 16.5 Craven Road Studio main doors open at night

17

Pool House

Koning Eizenberg

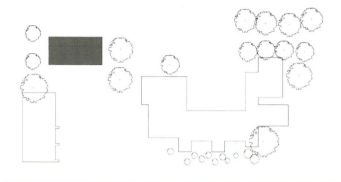

Pool House
Koning Eizenberg

South Pasadena, California   34.1°N, 118.2°W   2009

650 SF

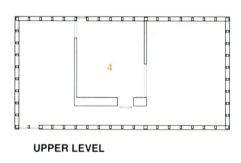

UPPER LEVEL

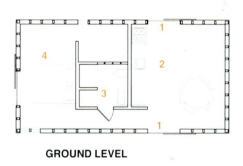

GROUND LEVEL

FLOOR PLANS
1 entry
2 kitchen
3 bathroom
4 bedroom

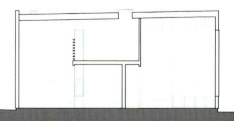

Figure 17.2 Pool House large sliding door leads to bedroom space

This simple two-story volume, now the pool house, served as a temporary dwelling for a family of four while the larger "compound of rooms" was built on a flag-shaped lot just northeast of Los Angeles. In addition to the small scope, the architects were also working within a tight time frame. The clients decided late in the project, just before demolition of the existing house was to begin, that they wanted to live on-site during the construction. The small house was designed and built in six months. The design had to be "both quick and cheap."[1]

The easy-going clients lived in the pool house for fourteen months with their two children, aged ten and twelve. They needed the space to be used in many ways over the years ahead. A central core of kitchen and bath separates the bedroom from the living space. The loft space, on top of the core, provides sleeping space for kids. This "space in flux" can be used as a pool house or an in-law suite or serve as part of the kids' domain.

The building uses few materials; or as Eizenberg likes to say, "there isn't much in it."[2] It is clad with a combination of white Kynar-finished aluminum panels and cellular polycarbonate panels outside, gypsum board or the backside of the polycarbonate panels on the inside. The floor is concrete and the roof deck, reached via a hatch, is covered in Astro turf for fun family picnics.

Light enters the building in two ways. Indirect light comes into areas through the translucent polycarbonate panels. Eizenberg wanted the space to be suffused by the light so inhabitants felt they were really "in the light." Direct light comes from fixed points that also offer views and access to the outside through 4-foot-wide sliding doors. The design team thought about how light moves from outside to inside and from inside to outside. During the day, the translucent panels allow diffuse light to permeate the interior. At night, those same panels transmit light to the exterior and the building glows like a lantern.

Figure 17.3 Pool House looking from loft to bedroom space

Designing a small house on a limited budget requires discipline to find the minimal means to get the maximum effect. Eizenberg reasoned that since light was free, she would design a house that was fully illuminated inside. She considers it the "anti-California modern house," one without maximum views to the garden. The material choices and light considerations are linked. The simple linear equation of less glass equals less views equals less openings equals less steel

results in a lower cost. Since polycarbonate is less expensive than glass, more polycarbonate was used, resulting in more diffuse light.

Eizenberg finds the steps for designing small projects are essentially the same as when designing larger buildings, but she looks for fewer classes of moves. In a larger project, the moves are scaled up. In the early days of this firm's practice,

Figure 17.4 Pool House view through the house with kitchenette on the right

the smaller projects were more about experimentation. In its current work, there is little distinction among projects of different scales. Each project offers a unique opportunity, regardless of scale.

Project scope does, however, determine detailing requirements. The durability of the detail needs to be more carefully investigated in a larger project, and more carefully

drawn. In a smaller project, with fewer details, the drawn form can be less precise because the architect has the opportunity to observe construction and resolve any potential detailing issues. The financial repercussions of any adjustments are much larger for big projects where the details are amplified and multiplied. Though the firm appreciates finely tuned details, they prefer details to have the appearance of a more casual attitude. They try to communicate an idea of

informality to make it look easy, as if no decision was made regarding the detail.

Eizenberg finds people have a tendency to fear what they are missing out on when they are designing a custom single-family house. She encourages her clients not to overthink the issues and to just build what is needed and not what *might* be needed. Providing one big space, a few smaller spaces, and the utility areas allows people to use those three types of spaces in different ways.

Koning Eizenberg, located in Los Angeles, has a very diverse practice that is rooted in the practical. They have a "body of work that demands to be understood as a series of practical solutions to the real problems of real people trying to live with dignity and grace."[3] The firm prefers to have clients work with a contractor for preconstruction services and preliminary pricing rather than competitive bid projects. The entire team can fine-tune the design to get the right fit of budget and scope. In a smaller project it is the same iterative process but with fewer pieces, classes of options, and less variety since less can fit in. Eizenberg is always measuring and double-checking

spaces to confirm how much room is needed between a chair and a wall or a built-in banquette. While she has a great deal of acquired knowledge about how much space something needs, she admits she is also neurotic about testing and questioning. The firm has a healthy respect for history yet finds it is more appropriate for references to be subliminal and accumulated over time rather than specific. History can be less intimidating if generalized than when it is looking at you directly.

Notes

1   Julie Eizenberg, interview with author. Los Angeles, California. January 2014.
2   Eizenberg.
3   William Mitchell, "Bound for Santa Monica Bay: An Introduction to the Work of Koning Eizenberg," in *Koning Eizenberg: Buildings*, Aaron Betsky and Julie Eizenberg (New York: Rizzoli International Publications, 1996, pp. 8–11), p. 8.

Figure 17.5 Pool House ladder to loft

18

Blossom Street 03

Nonya Grenader

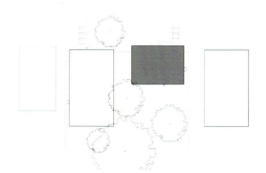

Blossom Street 03
Nonya Grenader

Houston, Texas   29.8°N, 95.4° W   2008

800 SF

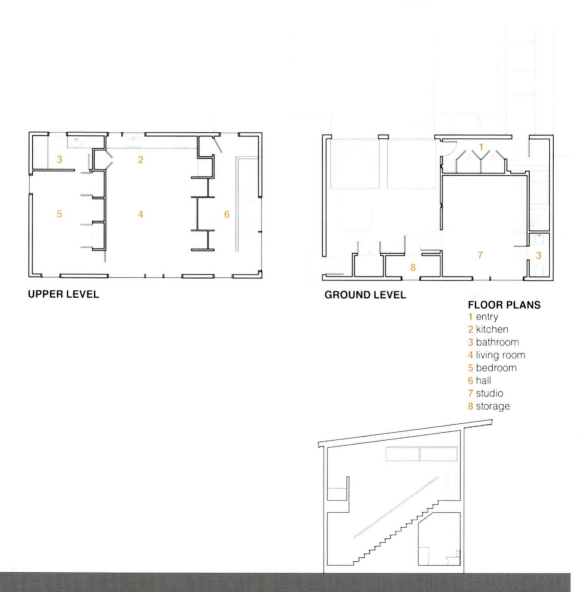

UPPER LEVEL

GROUND LEVEL

FLOOR PLANS
1 entry
2 kitchen
3 bathroom
4 living room
5 bedroom
6 hall
7 studio
8 storage

Figure 18.2 Blossom Street 03 south wall faces the garden

taut volumes create a syncopated composition, defending the street against the bulging developer-driven townhouses nearby.

This two-story dwelling places the main living spaces on the second floor above the double garage and a studio space that opens to the garden. Upstairs, a wide hallway can accommodate an office space, or even a guest room with a single bed for short-duration visits, in addition to the living, sleeping, and bathing spaces. The efficient circulation hugs the southern garden edge of the floor plan. The efficiency of space is matched with energy- and water-efficient fittings. The ceiling slopes up to the south, providing an intimate scale for the guest bed nook, increasing the spaciousness of the public area, and providing a surface to reflect warm southern light.

Light is essential in smaller houses and was especially important to the architect of this dwelling. Generous light can expand the feeling of the space, and both the number of sources and the orientation of light are critical. Varying the sources allows the light to animate the space; light quality and direction change the perception of everything else in the space. Grenader works in various media and often uses physical three-dimensional models to study light in a space, yet she has found that one can really only confirm the light quality once the building is complete.

The site, in a redeveloping neighborhood close to downtown Houston, is flat and relatively featureless, except for its proximity to the house next door. This portion of a double project is the "daughter" house for the adjacent "mother" house. The two houses, designed in tandem and in direct relationship to each other, create a coordinated front elevation. Each volume helps to define the exterior back garden, complete with a shuffleboard court for family tournaments. Both houses are compact and share some formal characteristics with a slightly earlier work next to the mother house, designed for the artist Jim Love. Together, the three

Grenader seeks to always find a palette within the budget range that is appropriate for the project. This house incorporates simple and direct materials, with each major material distributing light in a different way. Shadows and sunlight equally animate the hard-wearing galvanized panels on the tightly detailed exterior. The light-colored bamboo floor becomes almost dematerialized with direct sunlight. The great density of storage cabinetry, used as thickened dividers between rooms, is painted white to reflect indirect light throughout the house. A bright orange Silestone countertop in the kitchen provides a rectangle of color in an otherwise neutral space.

Figure 18.3 Blossom Street 03 bedroom with east wall storage divider

For Grenader, overhangs are a necessary requirement in Houston, where it rains 40 inches most years, to protect the building and its occupants from the rain and sun. The ceiling line follows a simple shed roof, which provides extensive southern overhangs for the compact volume. A suspended metal awning also protects the north-facing front door.

Most clients come to Grenader with economy in mind. These very real limits do focus the project, but the design process can be a slippery slope as portions of the project can keep getting bigger. She gently reminds clients that each additional foot of house equals one less foot of garden space. Extending the interior space to the exterior means you can also extend to a collective space, and small houses have to carefully calibrate issues of privacy and intimacy. There are a few tricks that Grenader uses to help stop "scope creep" such as utilizing outdoor spaces for circulation or having each space serve multiple functions. A carport can become a porch or, in this case, a wide hallway can be an office or a guest bedroom.

Grenader is the principal of her own firm, Nonya Grenader, FAIA. She also co-teaches the Rice Building Workshop (RBW) with Danny Samuels at Rice University and truly believes that an economy of means can equal elegance if you find that "just enough place."[1] A small project can incorporate just one or two special things and everything else needs to be quiet. Her work is often driven by the client's budget; she finds it can be even tougher to balance the budget when the overall scope of the project is smaller. Size limits do help to focus the project and force good decisions based on the continuous dance between pushing innovation and wanting the client to be satisfied for many years to come.

Grenader carries a sketchbook everywhere and is constantly looking at the world around her. She documents spaces she visits and notes their proportion, ceiling height, and light sources. She is particularly struck by the great choreography of use in the small cabin Le Corbusier designed in 1949 in Roquebrune-Cap-Martin along the southern coast of France. She often looks at vernacular precedents, such as southern row houses or the simple Cape Cod, which can expand as needed. She admires the modesty of shotgun houses and the power of repetition such as in the work of John Biggers—the painter who, in 1949, established the art department at what is now Texas Southern University.

Note

1   Nonya Grenader, interview with author. Houston, Texas. August 2012.

OPPOSITE TOP
Figure 18.4 Blossom Street 03 stairs with office and guest bed in hallway

OPPOSITE BELOW
Figure 18.5 Blossom Street 03 living room faces garden

19

Nested House

LOJO

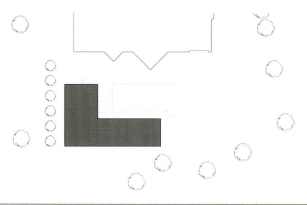

Nested House
LOJO Architecture

Houston, Texas   29.8°N, 95.4°W   2014

895 SF

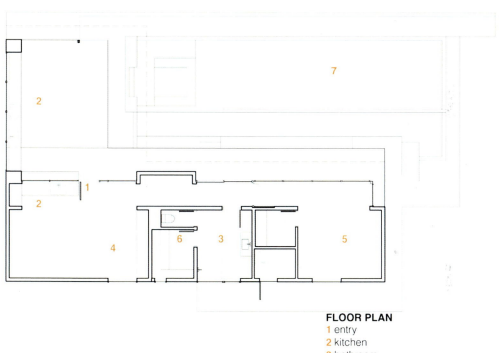

FLOOR PLAN
1 entry
2 kitchen
3 bathroom
4 living room
5 bedroom
6 sauna
7 future pool

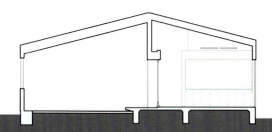

Figure 19.2 Nested House north elevation

This guesthouse on a large lot in a suburb west of Houston began as an even smaller project. The client, who is from Kazakhstan, originally requested a space similar to the saunas in his home country. The architects designed the house as a series of successive layers that nest the sauna within a bathroom and mechanical core at the center of the guesthouse. This core is located within a rectangular bar building, wrapped by an L-shaped outer layer that extends the living space and defines an outdoor kitchen and dining room. The building's configuration helps to frame an outdoor space and to deflect sound coming from a nearby freeway. A large bedroom on the east end of the building is separated from the living space by the central core and is reached by an elongated hall that stretches between the two ends. The living space is directly connected to the large covered outdoor kitchen that helps define the future garden and outdoor spa.

The standing-seam Galvalume panels on the roof extend down to clad the north and south walls. Each is a continuous piece of metal mechanically seamed on-site, stretching from the top of the roof to the base of the wall. All other exterior walls are wrapped with a Siberian larch rainscreen cladding held one and one-half inches from the vapor barrier. Siberia's short growing season results in a dense durable wood that is also naturally rot- and termite-resistant. The hard, dense wood, commonly used in Europe, has small, tight knots and takes stain well. Site-built maple interior cabinets and interior poplar trim both received a white wash to neutralize contrast with the interior painted walls. As a reference to the yurts of the client's country of origin, the architects clad the walls that enclose the bathroom and sauna with a milled 100 percent merino sheep wool from Germany called Fitz Felt. This makes the space both acoustically absorptive and softens the walls, while reminding the clients of their heritage. A cantilevered concrete slab, sealed for the interior floor, supports the entire building. Steel beams support the cantilever to make the transparent corner of glass in the bedroom hover over the garden below.

Daylight from a variety of directions layers light throughout the interior. North light is maximized by a big bank of windows, ensuring that artificial light would not be necessary

Figure 19.3 Nested House living room looking east towards felt clad wall

during daylight hours. Minimal south-facing windows reduce heat gain and sound transmission. Other windows wash the walls with light to further expand the sense of spaciousness. The ceiling follows the underside of the roof and slopes to a height of 14 feet at the north wall. This increased volume makes the interior feel more generous. A light shelf helps define that gained space, allowing the ceiling plan to be unpenetrated by any lighting or mechanical systems. At night, artificial light is bounced off the uninterrupted plane of the smooth ceiling.

Reduced reliance on built-in cabinetry reflects the client's culture of using freestanding furniture for storage. However, the architects cleverly designed niches to hold the furniture so they would not protrude into the space of the room. Limited kitchen cabinetry wraps around one outside corner of the

living area. A large pass-through window connects the interior cooking area with the large, covered outdoor kitchen and entertaining space. Fleetwood doors and glass panels along the north face visually connect the interior to the exterior, further expanding the feeling of spaciousness. The cooking porch is enclosed on three sides to both define the "outdoor room" and to help move the sound around the perimeter of the site.

The architecture firm LOJO was founded by Jason Logan and Matt Johnson in 2011 in Houston, Texas. Logan and Johnson use the same highly collaborative iterative process for designs regardless of project scale. Their challenge in a larger project is to maintain a clear idea and not overcomplicate the design with increased programmatic requirements. In smaller projects, they work hard to find the one idea that will

Figure 19.4 Nested House glass wraps around corner and north wall bringing in abundant natural light

drive everything. This project, characterized by the city as an "auxiliary building" because it is less than 900 square feet, also has fewer regulatory constraints.

The architects study airplane cabins and cars to learn ways to squeeze uses into every square inch. Johnson grew up sailing

and recalls the highly refined compactness of the below-deck cabin balancing with the vast domain of the ocean above deck. The architects admit, "even if you build something tiny and efficient and balance it with generous outdoor space, at some point you need to transform your life and simplify in general."[1]

Figure 19.5 Nested House outdoor kitchen and dining porch

Note

1   Jason Logan and Matt Johnson, interview with author.
    Houston, Texas. February 2014.

20

Envelope House

Bohlin Cywinski Jackson

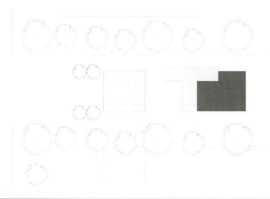

Envelope House
Bohlin Cywinski Jackson

Seattle, Washington   47.6°N, 122.3°W   2006

1000 SF

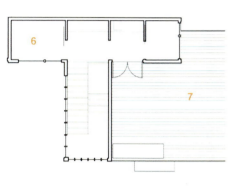

UPPER LEVEL - UNIT 2

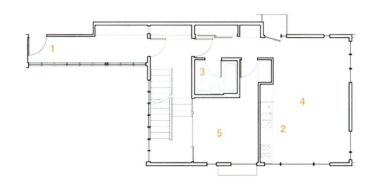

GROUND LEVEL - UNIT 2

FLOOR PLAN
1 entry
2 kitchen
3 bathroom
4 living/dining
5 bedroom
6 reading pod
7 deck

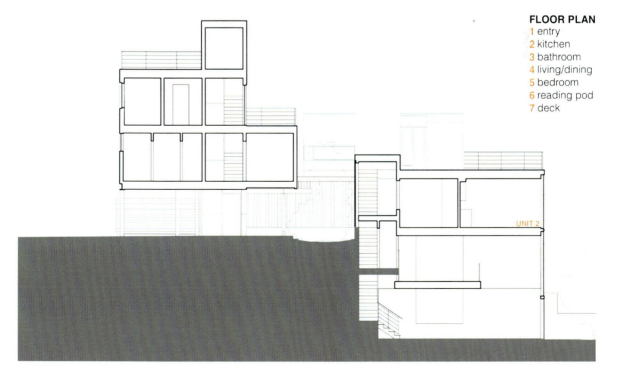

Figure 20.2 Envelope House design sketch

This multi-unit structure contains three small living units. The client, a landscape architect, requested a scheme that would maximize the investment potential on the narrow lot. The three units are distributed in two volumes that define a shared central courtyard on the sloped site in this rapidly changing neighborhood of Fremont, northwest of Lake Union in Seattle. The project, currently rented as three separate units, was designed to be flexible. The buildings can also be used as one or two residences. The owner intends to use one unit for her home and another for her studio.

Modest building materials with thoughtful details clearly communicate the assembly systems. The foundation and site walls are poured-in-place concrete. The forming technique is reflected in the rough texture of the finished walls. Exposed dimensional wood elements express the typical platform framing assembly system and are an economical way to introduce material warmth into the interior spaces. The exterior is clad with durable HardiePanel cement board panels with metal flashing expressing a horizontal pattern. Bright paint on the panels clarifies the volumes of the playful composition.

The courtyard separates the units, provides privacy for each home, and allows ample natural light into each compact unit on this tight site in a dense neighborhood. Translucent stair volumes flank the courtyard and bring light to the interior spaces while providing an additional layer of visual privacy for each unit's living spaces. Windows enliven the exterior composition and introduce light and views. The architects believe the location of openings is important, preferring corner windows rather than punched openings and extending

windows to the ceiling height to flood the ceiling plane with diffuse light. Projecting bay windows focus on views of Lake Union and the Seattle skyline.

In addition to typical living or sleeping spaces, each unit includes a reading pod or a loft. These small rooms, each enhanced with generously scaled windows for the diminutive spaces, can be used for a variety of purposes. Each unit also has a connection to an exterior space to further expand the available living space. One unit has a high balcony, another opens to a large roof deck, and the third has direct access to the ground-floor garden.

Choreographing the circulation, especially in a multi-unit building, is an important place to start the design. The architects balance circulation and privacy by rethinking the arrangement of elements. Circulation sequences might become more rapid and shorter in order to reveal different things along a path that is more fluid and has a looser structure. Most people can relate to a small house or remember how they shared space as college students. This can provide a new model for urban living where spaces are less defined, where only what is essential is provided, and the opportunistic aspect is explored.

The firm of Bohlin Cywinski Jackson, founded in 1965, has offices in Wilkes-Barre, Pittsburgh, Philadelphia, Seattle, and San Francisco. Each office works at all scales; and the architects find that, by working at various extremes of scale, projects can inform one other. Designing at both scales allows for considerations of spatial sequences and where functions overlap for sharing of space. Seattle office

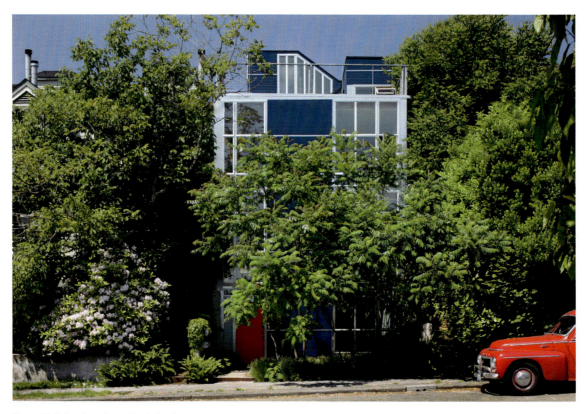

Figure 20.3 Envelope House street elevation

firm principals Robert Miller and Ray Calabro mention the Coleman camper, with its folding table that exists in the same space as the sleeping area, as a puzzle of negative space.[1] Being from a camping generation, they are nostalgic about the scale and inventive, transformative nature of those objects.

For smaller projects, the firm adjusts the size and organization of the project team. Sometimes design begins with a charette and a large group of designers tackling the problem for short periods. Other times they might stretch out the project over a long period of time to fit it into the gaps between larger commissions. The firm finds smaller projects a good way to look at a particular construction type or system and to help teach younger staff how a building goes together. As a busy firm principal, Miller finds that he can easily concentrate on smaller-scale problems in the limited space of an airplane's fold down table and within a limited flight time.[2]

OPPOSITE TOP
Figure 20.4 Envelope House interior view from stair with reading pod beyond

OPPOSITE BELOW
Figure 20.5 Envelope House dining room with full height window

Figure 20.6 Envelope House roof terrace

Notes

1 Ray Calabro and Robert Miller, interview with author.
   Seattle, Washington. July 2013.
2 Ray Calabro and Robert Miller.

List of Work

Variant ONE: POROUS DWELLINGS

1
Watershed
FLOAT
70 SF
2008
Wren, Oregon
44.6° N, 123.4° W
Project Team: Erin Moore
Photographer: J. Gary Tarleton

2
Music Box
John Grable Architects, Inc.
Size: 400 SF
Date: 2012
Location: Sisterdale, Texas
Latitude: 30.0° N, 98.7° W
Project Team: John Grable, FAIA, Matt Martinez
Photographer: John Grable, Matt Martinez
Builder: Truax Construction

3
False Bay Writer's Cabin
Olson Kundig Architects
500 SF
2010
San Juan Island, Washington State
48.5° N, 123.0° W
Project Team: Tom Kundig
Photographer: Tim Bies, Benjamin Benschneider
Builder: Lowe Construction

4
Ravine Guest House
Shim-Sutcliffe
500 SF
2004
Don Mills, Canada
43.7° N, 79.3° W
Project Team: Brigitte Shim and Howard Sutcliffe (principals)
    with Min Wang, Mark Graham (project team)
Photographer: James Dow, Raimund Koch
Builder: Tony Azevedo

5
Writer's Studio
Cooper Joseph Studio
525 SF
2007
Ghent, NY
42.3° N, 73.6° W
Project Team: Wendy Evans Joseph, Manan Shah, Robert Furno,
    Thruston Pettus, Farzana Gandhi
Photographer: Elliott Kaufman
Builder: Jim Romanchuk and Sons

6
Hill Country Jacal
Lake/Flato
925 SF
Date: 1997
Pipe Creek, Texas
29.7° N, 98.9° W
Project Team: Ted Flato, Eric Buch
Photographer: Leigh Christian
Builder: William Orr

7
Kemper Cabin
Suyama Peterson Deguchi
1,000 SF
1992
Skagit County, Washington
48.5° N, 121.8° W
Project Team: George Suyama
Photographer: David Story
Builder: Dale Brotherton

Variant TWO: FOCUSED DWELLINGS

8
Marfa 10×10
Candid Rogers Studio
320 SF
2007
Marfa, Texas
30.32° N, 104.0° W
Project Team: Candid Rogers, Gonzalo Fraga, Ayuko Hishikawa
Photographer: Chris Cooper, Candid Rogers (image in snow)
Builder: Quality Finishing

9
Keenan Tower House
Marlon Blackwell Architect
560 SF
2000
Fayetteville, Arkansas
36.1° N, 94.2° W
Project Team: Marlon Blackwell, FAIA (principal), Meryati Johari
     Blackwell, Dianne Meek, Phil Hadfield
Photographer: Timothy Hursley
Builder: Razorback Ironworks + Pizzini + Don Lourie

10
Sky Ranch
The Miller Hull Partnership
800 SF
2007
Seattle, Washington
47.6° N, 122.3° W
Project Team: Scott Wolf, Ron Rochon, Kiki Gram, and Grace
     Leong
Photographer: Benjamin Benschneider

11
Scholar's Library
GLUCK +
800 SF
2003
Upstate NY
Project Team: Peter L. Gluck, David Mabbott,
     Frederick Rissom
Photographer: Paul Warchol, Erik Freeland
Builder: GLUCK+

12
Roland Cabin
David Salmela
810 SF
2009
La Pointe, Wisconsin
46.8° N, 90.8° W
Project Team: David Salmela
Photographer: Peter Bastianelli-Kerze
Builder: Northwoods Construction

13
Small House in an Olive Grove
Cooper Joseph Studio
850 SF
2010
Geyserville, California
38.7° N, 122.9° W
Project Team: Wendy Evans Joseph, Chris Cooper, Chris Good,
    Michael Walch, Reed Langworthy, Farzana Gandhi
Photographer: Elliott Kaufman
Builder: Redhorse Constructors Inc.

14
Stacked Cabin
Johnsen Schmaling Architects
880 SF
2012
Muscoda, Wisconsin
43.2° N, 90.5° W
Project Team: Brian Johnsen and Sebastian Schmaling
Photographer: John J. Macaulay
Builder: Hansen Builders

Variant THREE: PROTECTED DWELLINGS

15
Williams Cabin
Atkinson Architecture
290 SF
2008
Durango, Colorado
37.3° N, 107.9° W
Project Team: Stephen Atkinson
Photographer: Mika Fowler
Builder: Steve Kawell

16
Craven Road Studio
Shim-Sutcliffe
560 SF
2006
Toronto, Ontario
43.7° N, 79.4° W
Project Team: Brigitte Shim and Howard Sutcliffe (principals),
    with Michael Goorevich (project architect)
Photographer: Bob Gundu, Finn O'Hara
Builder: Derek Nicholson Inc.

17
Pool House
Koning Eizenberg
650 SF
2009
South Pasadena, California
34.1° N, 118.2° W
Project Team: Julie Eizenberg (Principal In Charge),
    Oonagh Ryan (Project Manager/Project Architect), Keith
    Gendel (Designer), CW Howe Associates (Structural
    Engineer)
Photographer: Eric Staudenmaier
Builder: William Kent Development, Inc.

18
Blossom Street 03
Nonya Grenader
800 SF
2008
Houston, Texas
29.8° N, 95.4° W
Project Team: Nonya Grenader FAIA, Christopher Mechaley,
    Sam Grenader
Photographer: Nash Baker
Builder: Mainland Construction /Gary Inman

19
Nested House
LOJO
895 SF
2014
Houston, Texas
29.8° N, 95.4° W
Project Team: Jason Logan, Matt Johnson, Josh Robins
Photographer: Luis Ayala
Builder: Streva Construction

20
Envelope House
Bohlin Cywinski Jackson
1000 SF – three units
2006
Seattle, Washington
47.6° N, 122.3° W
Project Team: Robert Miller, Peter Bohlin, Daniel Ralls
Photographer: Nic Lehoux
Builder: Albion Group

Figure Credits

12.5 Peter Bastianelli-Kerze

13.1 Elliot Kaufman

13.2 Elliot Kaufman

13.3 Elliot Kaufman

13.4 Elliot Kaufman

13.5 Elliot Kaufman

14.1 John J. Macaulay

14.2 John J. Macaulay

14.3 John J. Macaulay

14.4 John J. Macaulay

14.5 John J. Macaulay

15.1 Gunnar Conrad

15.2 Mika Fowler

15.3 Mika Fowler

15.4 Mark Williams

15.5 Mika Fowler

16.1 Bob Gundu

16.2 Bob Gundu

16.3 Finn O'Hara

16.4 Bob Gundu

16.5 Finn O'Hara

17.1 Eric Staudenmaier

17.2 Eric Staudenmaier

17.3 Eric Staudenmaier

17.4 Eric Staudenmaier

17.5 Eric Staudenmaier

18.1 Nash Baker

18.2 Nash Baker

18.3 Nash Baker

18.4 Nash Baker

18.5 Nash Baker

19.1 Luis Ayala

19.2 Luis Ayala

19.3 Luis Ayala

19.4 Luis Ayala

19.5 Luis Ayala

20.1 Nic Lehoux

20.3 Nic Lehoux

20.4 Nic Lehoux

20.5 Nic Lehoux

20.6 Nic Lehoux

Index

Page references for illustrations are in italics.